THE NATIVITY

DOUBLEDAY

New York
London
Toronto
Sydney
Auckland

The
NATIVITY

History
&
Legend

GEZA VERMES

PUBLISHED BY DOUBLEDAY

Copyright © 2006 by Geza Vermes

All Rights Reserved

Originally published in England by Penguin Books Ltd., London, 2006.
This edition published by arrangement with Penguin Books Ltd.

Published in the United States by Doubleday,
an imprint of The Doubleday Broadway Publishing Group,
a division of Random House, Inc., New York.

www.doubleday.com

DOUBLEDAY and the portrayal of an anchor with a dolphin
are registered trademarks of Random House, Inc.

Book design by Elizabeth Rendfleisch

Library of Congress Cataloging-in-Publication Data

Vermès, Géza, 1924–
The Nativity : history and legend / Geza Vermes. — 1st U.S. ed.
p. cm.
Includes bibliographical references and index.
1. Jesus Christ—Nativity. 2. Christmas. I. Title.
BT315.3. V47 2007
232.92—dc22   2007025588
ISBN 978-0-385-52241-0

PRINTED IN THE UNITED STATES OF AMERICA

1 3 5 7 9 10 8 6 4 2

First U.S. Edition

Contents

THE NATIVITY

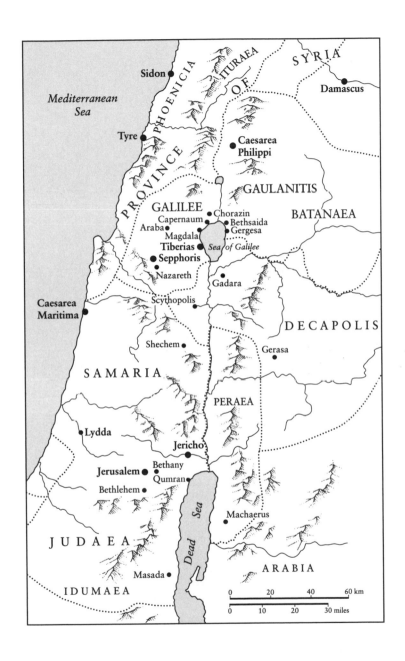

Palestine in the age of Jesus

Prologue

Old Christmas—New Christmas

———

Christmas is no longer what it used to be. It has lost its religious significance in many parts of the Western world and has become the climax of a season of overspending, overeating, and uncontrolled merrymaking. The new Christmas mirrors its pagan predecessor, which celebrated the winter solstice. Christmas is the children's favorite festival of the year, and for the grown-ups it is a time for indulging in sweet old-time memories.

My earliest recollections take me back further than I care to think, to the happy days before the Second World War. I was four years old. My parents, like many assimilated Hungarian Jews before Hitler appeared on the horizon, wanted their little boy to share the seasonal jollification of their Christian friends and neighbors. (Today in progressive Jewish circles the Festival of Lights, or Hanukkah, has become a substitute Christmas, humorously nicknamed Hanukmas, Chrismukkah or Chrisnukkah.) Hungarian children in those days believed that Christmas presents were brought to them by the Little

Jesus, or *Jézuska*, who made his rounds on the evening of December 24, and placed the gifts under the decorated Christmas tree, which was delivered from heaven by little angels. I was warned to resist curiosity, for should I peep into the sitting room from my quarters, the angels would be frightened away and that would be goodbye to presents and sweets. I remember how greatly I was tempted to investigate the noises coming from the living room while I was having my afternoon siesta, but wise by nature from the start, I overcame temptation. Then in the evening I was allowed to enter. What a glorious sight it was: the tree with its real candles and little sparklers, which burst into hundreds of bright stars when lit with a match. And there were presents galore, more than I could count. Singing was heard from the street. The doorbell rang and a group of working-class children inquired whether they might bring in their "Bethlehem," a cardboard crib in which Mary, Joseph, and Jesus shared the stable with an ox and a donkey. One of the boys carried the star of Bethlehem on a rod, and other children played the angels, the shepherds, and the three kings. Their labor was rewarded with bits of chocolate and a few pennies. Everything was charming and delightful; a naive religious aura filled the place. The red-suited Santa Claus or Father Christmas did not exist. We had "Uncle" or "Saint" Nicholas instead, who visited the children much earlier in the month, on the evening of December 5, and stuffed their stockings with goodies. To teach them not to misbehave, he beat with a stick a young companion who played the devil.

A year later matters became slightly more sophisticated in the Vermes household. By then I had learned how to write with capital letters from the headlines of the many newspapers which filled our home, and I used the newly acquired skill to provide "little Jesus" with a list of toys and books I hoped he would supply. My father, a journalist, put the letter, addressed to "Jesus in heaven," into his jacket pocket and promised to drop it into the mailbox at the street corner a few days before Christmas. Then catastrophe struck. I did something naughty, I can no longer remember what, and my father decided to teach me a lesson. He fiddled with the knobs of his primitive radio set, his means of communication with the upper world, and to my utmost consternation, he pulled my letter out of his pocket. To punish me for my mischief, little Jesus returned the message to the sender. I burst into tears and firmly promised to amend my ways. Pardon was granted and the much-hoped-for presents somehow materialized.

My wife's early Christmas recollections are of a quite different kind. Though numbering a Jew among her great-grandparents, she grew up in Cracow in a strictly Polish Catholic setting. In her world, Christmas was not associated with *large* presents. Those had been delivered by Saint Nicholas during the night of December 5. (I remember from my student days that in Belgium, too, Saint Nicholas was the chief gift giver, and I gather that in the Netherlands children expect this benevolent ancient bishop of Myra from Asiatic Turkey to arrive by ship from Spain.) The Christmas pleasure of Polish youngsters came from preparing the Christmas tree and attaching to it sweets, oranges, apples, and shiny baubles. Less pleasurable were the duties imposed on them by their parents to apologize for all the naughtiness of the past year—promising that they would be well behaved in the future—and to convey specific good wishes to each member of the family. But then came the crowning glory of Christmas Eve, a sumptuous meal of twelve courses, accompanied—in other Polish families—by large doses of alcohol among the grown-ups, many of whom found themselves under the influence by the time they had to set off to church to attend midnight mass.

As he remembers it, the experience of the junior member of the family, Ian Vermes, born in Oxford in 1990, does not resemble either mine or his mother's. In the true British way, his Christmas was celebrated on December 25 and not on Christmas Eve, as was the case on the continent. At the age of three and a half he was waiting with burning excitement for the moment when on Christmas morning he could burst into the sitting room and rip the shiny wrapping paper off the many presents left for him, not by little Jesus but by an avuncular white-bearded Santa Claus. The Christmas tree, adorned not with wax candles but with electric lights, held no mystery for him. He never heard that it had been brought to him by angels: he himself helped the previous day to prepare it. A year later even the Father Christmas mystique suffered a deadly blow. Ian, unable to withstand curiosity, quietly crept downstairs from his bedroom late in the evening of December 24 and discovered his mother and me wrapping up the presents and placing them under the Christmas tree. For years he continued to pretend that he believed in Father Christmas, and sent him detailed shopping lists, stating the exact price of the various items in order to ensure that Santa had with him enough money to make all the purchases. His Christmas had become like that of most children in these days: the expectation of toys, videos, DVDs, and computer games as seen advertised day in, day out, on television. Now at the age of sixteen he likes to think of himself as an agnostic scientist and claims that he has never associated Christmas with anything religious. December 25 is simply the great day of the increasingly lavish annual bonanza.

But what actually lies behind the feast of the Nativity? To discover the origins of Christmas, we must examine the main records that the New Testament places at our disposal—the Infancy Gospels of Matthew and Luke—and endeavor to squeeze the truth out of them. This truth, as we shall see, belongs only very slightly to history and mostly derives from man's hopeful and creative religious imagination.

The Nativity in Christian Imagination and in the Gospels

❧✦❦✦❧

THERE ARE THREE VERSIONS OF THE Nativity play. Churchgoers of all ages are familiar with the first. It is regularly sketched, Christmas after Christmas, in sermons preached from the pulpit. It can be found and admired on the great Nativity canvases lovingly created by Christian artists over the centuries. One sees a bearded old man walking beside a donkey on whose back a heavily pregnant young woman rides. The towers of Bethlehem are faintly visible in the distance. In the crowded city the inns are packed, and Joseph, after much toing and froing and searching, can discover only a modest shed in the neighborhood for Mary to give birth to her son. The newborn Jesus is laid by his mother in the manger between a cow and an ass. Old

Joseph observes the scene with benevolent and detached admi-
ration. Local shepherds are alerted by an angel and learn about
the arrival in the world of the Savior of the Jews. Soon three
kings approach, robed in glorious apparel. They have been led
from the far-distant Orient via Jerusalem to Bethlehem by a
mysterious star. At the royal palace they inquire where the recently born king of the Jews can be seen. First no one knows.
So on the advice of experts summoned by Herod, the kings are
sent to Bethlehem and with the help of the reappearing star
they find the stable, greet and worship Jesus, and offer him re-
gal presents. The curtain falls: end of act one.

Like a child's fairy tale, the Christmas story consists of an
admixture of the charming and the dreadful. In act two, generally not featured in Nativity plays, sweetness and joy suddenly
vanish and disaster looms on the horizon when bloodthirsty
Herod enters the fray. Realizing that the kings have tricked
him and slipped out of the country, Herod lets loose his cruel
soldiers on the infant boys of Bethlehem. They all perish—
from newborn babes to toddlers—except the child who has
made Herod so anxious.

Suddenly the scene changes again. Joseph falls asleep and
dreams of an angel, who sounds the alarm: father, mother, and
child must flee at once. Again we see the old man on the road,
accompanied by his faithful donkey, but this time it carries
the baby and his mother. Cleverly avoiding Herod's frontier
guards, they escape from Judaea and reach the safe haven of
Egypt, the land of the Nile.

In the last act the scenario gets slightly bogged down. The
final phases of the drama become hazy. We are presented with
the circumcision of Jesus and with his presentation in the

Temple of Jerusalem, but we do not learn when these things happened in relation to the escape to Egypt. Nor are the reason and the time of Jesus' move to peaceful Galilee and a happy childhood specified.

The Christian mind does not seem to be greatly bothered by these matters. Its perspective is compact and its chronological framework is foreshortened. For the ordinary faithful all the happenings are squeezed together between Christmas and Candlemas. According to the liturgy of the Church, Jesus was born on December 25. The innocents of Bethlehem were murdered three days later. Jesus was circumcised on January 1. In my Oxford University diary New Year's Day is still designated as the feast of the circumcision, but sadly in the Roman Catholic missals, revised after the Second Vatican Council, a solemnity of Mary, Mother of God, has been substituted for the old Latin rite's *Circumcisio Domini* (the circumcision of the Lord), and in consequence the Gospel reading "And at the end of eight days, when he was circumcised, he was called Jesus" has disappeared from the day's service. Jesus and Mary (and maybe Joseph) visited the Temple on February 2. So the Egyptian episode must have taken place between late December and the beginning of February, and the trip to Galilee immediately followed. Everything becomes neat and tidy except . . . most of this is legend or fiction.

With all due respect to Christian tradition, some of the essentials of the extended Christmas complex are a million miles away from fact and reality. For instance, the chances that Jesus was born on December 25 are 1 in 365 (or 366 in leap years). This date was invented by the Western church—as late as the fourth century under the emperor Constantine—as a way to replace the pagan festival of the Unvanquished Sun, and is first attested, to be precise, in a Roman calendar in AD 334.[1] Most Eastern Christians celebrate Jesus' birth or manifestation to the world on the feast of Epiphany (January 6), while according to the second-century Church Father Clement of Alexandria, other oriental communities commemorated the event on April 21 or May 20 (*Stromateis* [Miscellanea] 1:21).

In our search for clarification, let us begin by eliminating the three features of the traditional depiction of Christmas which are without written antecedents in the New Testament. Try as you may, you will find nothing in the Gospels to suggest that Joseph, repeatedly referred to as the father of Jesus, was an old man. We know nothing about his age, when he was born, or even when he died. The idea of an elderly Joseph derives from an apocryphal Gospel, the Protoevangelium of James the Brother of the Lord. In it he is described as a widower of advanced years who had sons and daughters from a previous marriage. These are then the members of the household of Joseph and Mary, whom the New Testament designates as the brothers and sisters of Jesus.

Neither do the Gospels contain any allusion to the friendly beasts, the ox and the ass, sharing the stable with Jesus. The imagery of these animals is borrowed from the prophet Isaiah, "The ox knows its owner, and the ass its master's crib; but Israel does not know, my people does not understand" (Isa 1:3). The Church saw in this passage the prefiguration of the later rejection of Christ by the Jewish people.

Finally, the New Testament nowhere suggests that the oriental visitors who followed the star to Bethlehem were kings.

The Greek text of Matthew designates them not as rulers or even "wise men," but as *magoi*, "Magi" or magicians (see p. 99). The upgrading of these eastern astrologers to the royal dignity is due to another artificial association of an Old Testament text with this episode of the Infancy Gospel. A passage taken from the Book of Isaiah reads, "And nations shall come to your light, and kings to the brightness of your rising" (Isa 60:3). It is completed by another verse a few lines further down in the same chapter of the same book, "They shall bring gold and frankincense, and shall proclaim the praise of the Lord" (Isa 60:6). Nor is it anywhere written that there were *three* kings. This figure is no doubt deduced from the number of gifts listed in Matthew, "gold and frankincense and myrrh" (Mt 2:11), with the assumption that one present was offered by each visitor.

The two other Christmas pictures are inspired by the New Testament. The first, arising from Matthew's Infancy narrative, begins with the genealogical table of Jesus (Mt 1:1–17) and is followed by Joseph's intention to divorce the pregnant Mary (Mt 1:18–19). His plan is altered when he is reassured by an angel in a dream that his fiancée's condition is due to the miraculous intervention of the Holy Spirit (Mt 1:20). Indeed, the virgin birth is the fulfillment of a prophecy of Isaiah (Mt 1:22–23). Joseph gives credence to this dream-revelation, marries Mary, and takes her to his home (Mt 1:24–25).

Jesus' arrival in this world is marked by the apparition of a star on the eastern horizon which leads the "wise men" of the Orient to Jerusalem (Mt 2:1–2). They go to the royal palace to find out the whereabouts of the newly born king of the Jews

(Mt 2:3). The astounded Herod consults the Jewish chief priests, who identify Bethlehem as the predicted birthplace of the expected Messiah in conformity with a prophecy by Micah 5:2 (Mt 2:4–6). Herod then extracts from the Magi the time of the first apparition of the star and cannily requires them to share with him whatever they learn about the child (Mt 2:7–8). With the help of the star, the Magi find Jesus and pay homage to him before, in accordance with the instruction they receive in a dream, they return home without retracing their steps to Jerusalem (Mt 2:9–12).

Once more Joseph is instructed by an angel in yet another dream to promptly take Jesus to Egypt in order to escape the massacre of the male children of Bethlehem, decreed by the jealous and enraged Herod, in fulfillment of the prophecy about Rachel, the wife of the Patriarch Jacob, lamenting the loss of her children in Jeremiah 31:15 (Mt 2:13–18). On the death of the king, the same angel, in a penultimate dream, orders Joseph to return to the land of Israel, thus bringing to realization another prediction (Hos 11:1), which announces that God will call his Son out of Egypt (Mt 2:19–21). However, when Joseph learns that Archelaus has succeeded Herod, his father, in Jerusalem, a final dream revises the previous instruction and directs him to take up residence in Galilee. An unidentified prophecy, "He shall be called a Nazarene," is cited to explain Jesus' association with Nazareth (Mt 2:22–23).

In the third version of the events of the Nativity, Luke has a substantially different story to tell. It contains two annunciations. In the first, the elderly priest Zechariah, resident in Judaea, is informed by the angel Gabriel that his aged and sterile wife, Elizabeth, will miraculously give birth to a son, John the Baptist (Lk 1:5–25). This is followed by a further message by the same Gabriel to Mary, an engaged virgin living in Nazareth, that she will conceive and bear Jesus, and that it is no more difficult for God to make her pregnant and keep her a virgin than to allow her kinswoman Elizabeth to give birth to a son in her old age (Lk 1:26–38). Mary at once visits Elizabeth in Judaea and stays with her until the birth of John the Baptist (Lk 1:39–80). She then travels back to Nazareth, only to take to the road again within a few weeks. The census ordered by the emperor Augustus is given as the explanation of the journey of Joseph and Mary to Bethlehem, where Jesus is born in an animal shelter outside the city of David, the town's hostels being filled to the brim by crowds of people arriving to register (Lk 2:1–7). The newborn child is greeted by local shepherds, and by a heavenly choir singing glory to God (Lk 2:8–20). Eight days later, in conformity with Jewish law, Jesus is circumcised, and on the fortieth day following his birth he is taken to the Temple and the ceremony of the redemption of the firstborn is performed, while his mother completes the purification ritual obligatory after giving birth to a male offspring. In the sanctuary Jesus is recognized by two old worshippers as the Messiah of the Jews and the redeemer of the Gentiles (Lk 2:25–38). Their religious duties accomplished, Joseph, Mary, and the infant immediately return to Nazareth, their original hometown (Lk 2:39–40).

The nature of the material determines the form that our investigation will take. Matthew and Luke seldom furnish the same information in the same order. Sometimes the themes are

of the birth of Jesus or of his family background and early life. The same is true about the Gospel of John, finally formulated probably in the first decade of the second century, give or take a few years. It has nothing to convey about the earthly beginnings of Christ, except that in some way they were connected to the ministry of a man named John—John the Baptist—but supplies in its magnificent prologue a mystical-philosophical insight into the eternal pre-existence of the *Logos*, the creative Word of God, that in the fullness of time and for a brief moment appeared in human shape in the person of Jesus to reveal God to mankind.

Matthew and Luke, whose Gospels are thought to have been published in the final two decades of the first century (AD 80–100), appended their birth stories as an introductory supplement to their compilation. The Infancy Gospels stand on their own. All four evangelists begin their main story with an adult Jesus (in his thirties, according to Lk 3:23), coming from nowhere and suddenly stepping into the limelight in AD 29, in the fifteenth year of the emperor of Rome, Tiberius.

In chronicling Jesus' infancy, Matthew and Luke agree only on a few basic points. The names of the protagonists are the same. The place of birth, the date, and the permanent address of the family are identical in both accounts. They also claim, each in his own way, that the pregnancy of Mary was out of the ordinary. But on most other details they completely differ.

Regarding the contradictions between Matthew and Luke, the names of the ancestors of Jesus are irreconcilable. The original place of residence of the parents is the Galilean Nazareth in Luke, but apparently the Bethlehem of Judaea in Matthew.

The extraordinary conception of Jesus through the Holy Spirit is announced only to Joseph in Matthew, and only to Mary in Luke. In Matthew, Joseph's first thought on noticing that Mary is expecting a child is that she has misbehaved, hence his intention to divorce her. There is no question in Matthew of Jesus being born in an improvised shelter. The family is found by the wise men in a *house* in Bethlehem. Only Matthew reports the apparition of a prodigious star, the visit of the Magi and the vicious intervention of Herod, the flight of the Holy Family to Egypt and their subsequent choice of Nazareth in Galilee as their permanent place of residence. A final distinctive mark of Matthew's infancy narrative is the presence of five biblical proof texts, Old Testament quotations introduced to demonstrate that in the events connected with the birth of Jesus biblical prophecies have been realized. The first of these—"Behold, a virgin shall conceive" (Isa 7:14 in Mt 1:23)—is of crucial importance.

Peculiar to Luke is the account relating to John the Baptist. This consists of the annunciation by the angel Gabriel of Mary's pregnancy in Nazareth, the travel of Mary from Galilee to Judaea to visit Elizabeth, the census bringing Joseph and Mary from Nazareth to Bethlehem, the birth of Jesus in a stable, the greeting of the newborn by shepherds and angels, the circumcision of Jesus and his presentation in the Temple, and the return of the family from Jerusalem to their home in Nazareth. Further sections belonging to Luke's special material are the three hymns, known as the Magnificat, the Benedictus, and the Nunc Dimittis, sung respectively by Mary or Elizabeth, Zechariah, and Simeon.

Since religious authority dislikes contradictions in its au-

thoritative texts, efforts have been deployed from the early
centuries of the Christian era by the official revisers and commentators of the Gospels to eliminate the manifest discrepancies between the infancy narratives of Matthew and Luke. A
good example of this unifying tendency is exhibited in the
Diatessaron or Gospel harmony, a combination of the four
Gospels into a single narrative, compiled by the second-century
author Tatian, a native of Assyria (Northern Iraq). In his version of the events, he first reproduces Luke's account of the
birth and circumcision of Jesus and the visit of mother and
child to Jerusalem. Then he records the arrival of the Magi, the
violent action of Herod, and the precipitate trip of the Holy
Family to Egypt. The *Diatessaron* failed to supplant the four
Gospels, and at the end the separate narratives triumphed,
notwithstanding the problems generated by their contradictions. To attempt a full reconciliation of the two Infancy
Gospels is a patently lost cause: squaring the circle would be
easier than reducing the two into a single coherent unity.

In view of all the complications, discrepancies, and contradictions displayed in the two infancy narratives, without men-
tioning the substantial number of legendary features contained
in them (dreams, angels, a miraculous star, etc.), it is not surprising that they have been a subject of concern for the representatives of the common Christian tradition in modern times
more than in antiquity. They have worried not only the liter-
alist or fundamentalist interpreters of the New Testament, but
also pious scholars who felt duty-bound to uphold the teaching
of the Church. They have all been struggling to produce a
smooth and unified version, which they have achieved only at
a price. These exegetes have been happy to settle the problem

of the virginal conception by simply calling it a miracle. They have tried to identify the star of Bethlehem as a genuine comet, falling star, or meteor. In the not too far distant past, we quite often encountered around Christmas in the columns of the newspapers academics, no doubt steeped in science but unquestionably ignorant of ancient literature, who advanced with great conviction half-baked "definitive" solutions of the dilemma. In the twenty-first century, their discoveries would be publicized in television documentaries in which a computer-reconstructed course of the star of the Magi would be presented as the ultimate optical proof.

As for the census ordered, according to Luke, by the emperor Augustus and administered by Quirinius, self-appointed defenders of Gospel truth still try to find ways and means to fit it into the end period of the reign of Herod the Great. It seems that sailing between Scylla and Charybdis proves as hazardous today as it used to be in olden times.

Let me select a few typical examples of exegetical acrobatics. In connection with the virgin birth, C. E. B. Cranfield, the noted Protestant New Testament scholar, has committed a double faux pas. First, he has presented the issue upside down and has stressed that "up to the present no proof of its *non-historicity* has been produced,"[2] as though the historicity of the virginal conception could be presumed and non-historicity is the alternative that requires demonstration. Furthermore, he has used his editorial authority to compel the liberal-minded authors of the relevant volume of the reputable series *International Critical Commentary* to water down the main concluding remark on chapter 2 of the Gospel of Matthew, which they have declared to be "not the stuff out of which history is made." Under duress, the two renowned writers W. D. Davies and Dale C. Allison were obliged to add: "But as the New Testament editor, Dr. Cranfield, urges, the readers should note that other critical scholars reckon with the possibility that the narratives contained in this section . . . may have much more substantial factual basis than is envisaged here."[3] Earlier the commentary on Matthew 1:18–25 carries an additional paragraph in parentheses: "(We are aware—and the NT editor of this series, Dr. Cranfield, has reminded us of this— that other competent critical scholars are firmly convinced of the historicity of the Virginal Conception, though not, of course, supposing that it can be conclusively proved by historico-critical methods, and that careful attention should be paid to their discussions of the relevant evidence as well as to the view expressed here)."[4]

Catholic students of the infancy narratives of Matthew and Luke seem to be particularly stretched between their wish to appear scholarly yet not to undermine cherished and binding beliefs of their Church concerning the miraculous conception of Jesus and the perpetual virginity of Mary.

Thus John P. Meier, in his monumental work *A Marginal Jew: Rethinking the Historical Jesus*, comforts his readers with the thought that regarding the reliability of the Nativity accounts "*total* skepticism is not in order" (vol. I, p. 205). They are told that stories about angelic annunciations and miraculous births should be taken "seriously," though not "*necessarily* . . . literally." Also they are reassured that the tradition concerning the virginal conception does not represent a "*late* legend" (my italics in all three quotations).

For scholarly Catholic ecclesiastics equivocation seems to

be the name of the game. The late Raymond Brown—whose monumental book *The Birth of the Messiah* (1977), which runs to 752 pages and is greatly respected by many—is the primary example of the position of "having your cake and eating it." He recognizes that angelic appearances, virginal conception, and the marvelous star are "patently legendary themes," that Matthew and Luke contradict each other, and that neither account is likely to be truly historical. But when it comes to the crunch, he opts for what he admits to be a "retrogressively conservative" position and is willing to shock his progressive critics even more by affirming that it is easier to explain the New Testament evidence of the virginal conception by positing a historical basis for it than by accepting it as pure theological creation. No surprise that in reviewing *The Birth of the Messiah* the celebrated literary scholar Frank Kermode has attributed Brown's refusal to acknowledge the made-up character of Matthew's birth story to his eagerness to secure the Catholic Church's imprimatur for his book. Hence the ironical conclusion: "Giving up the virgin birth might be bad for people."[5]

Other Christian scholars have felt no reluctance to call a spade a spade. In the considered judgment of Rudolf Bultmann, one of the greatest New Testament exegetes of the last century, the original Semitic report of Matthew's Infancy Gospel contained nothing about the virgin birth. It was a motif unheard of in the Jewish environment of the age, he stated, and it was first added to the Gospel account in the course of its transformation in Hellenism.[6] More recently, one of the most respected Jesus scholars, E. P. Sanders, also asserted without the slightest hesitation that the birth narratives are "the clearest cases of invention" in the Gospels.[7] As for the saying "I wouldn't put it past God to arrange a virgin birth if He wanted, but I very much doubt if He would," it is attributed, genuine or apocryphal, to David Jenkins, the outspoken former Anglican bishop of Durham.

In my recent book *The Passion* (Penguin, 2005), devoted to the study of the trial and crucifixion of Jesus, I played the detective who had to confront issues of real history on the basis of ancient literary evidence. I tried to determine the relation of the New Testament story to Jewish and Roman court procedures in first-century Palestine, and to evaluate the reliability of the Gospel portraits of Pilate and Caiaphas compared to parallel Jewish and Roman sources. Facing the Infancy Gospels, writer and reader find themselves in a quite different world. Here the independent investigator's duty is to deal with the birth stories in the Gospels in the same way as he would deal with any other problem of the history of religions. His first task is to sift the evidence and separate morsels of fact from legendary accretions. This done, it will be possible to gain an insight into the genesis, purpose, and significance of the religious ideas surrounding the birth of Jesus, a Jewish child who was first to be proclaimed the Messiah of Israel, then the Son of God, before rising even higher up on the ladder and being worshipped as God the Son, the Second Person of the Most Holy Trinity.

There is only one safe method to approach an ancient text such as the infancy narrative. We will have to begin with textual interpretation, the analysis of the evidence, verse by verse, line by line, and when necessary word by word. The findings of this investigation will then be compared with all the relevant information assembled from the parallel Jewish documents, biblical and postbiblical, and from the sources of classical literature and history. It is only after the establishment of the significance of the details that we will be able to penetrate the meaning of the New Testament story of the Nativity, which in time evolved into the religious complex called Christmas.

| 3 |

The Genealogies of Jesus

THE BIBLE IS FULL OF FAMILY TREES which strike most readers—apart from addicts of genealogical research—as far from fascinating, not to say plain boring. Yet they can be rich in meaning and in their variations reveal secret purposes. Scriptural genealogies have a threefold significance. When paraphrased, they may serve as an abridged account of history, but can also be used for two practical, legal purposes. The first of these is to demonstrate the legitimacy of kings and priests. Evidence of direct descent from the house of David was indispensable for succession to the throne and, as we will discover from the Infancy Gospels of Matthew and Luke, for the establishment of someone's Messianic status. It was also essential for a Jewish priest, holding a hereditary office handed down from father to son, to be able to prove that he belonged to a family which could trace its line back to Aaron in the tribe of Levi. Without such a pedigree he would lose his livelihood and would not be permitted to function in the Temple of Jerusalem. A genealogical table could also be useful in contested cases of inheritance, that is, when someone claimed entitlement to ancestral property.

As a rule, scriptural genealogies follow the male line, going from father to son. The most elaborate biblical list can be found in the First Book of the Chronicles. No less than nine chapters at the beginning of the book purport to record human and Jewish history starting with Adam, that is to say, in biblical terms from the creation, and going as far as the family of Saul, the first king of Israel, which in our terminology is the end of the eleventh century BC. As one may expect, genealogies usually proceed in a descending order. At the head of the list stands the patriarch, the first forebear of the group, and the family tree descends from father to son in a monotonous sequence of "begettings." Sometimes, however, a variation is introduced in that the chronicler reverses the order, beginning at the end and ending with the beginning. For instance, the genealogy of the great post-exilic priestly leader Ezra, who flourished in the fifth century BC, is traced back from him to the brother of Moses, Aaron, who probably lived some eight hundred years earlier in the thirteenth century BC (Ezra 7:1–5). These few snippets of information will come in useful when we turn to the two genealogies of Jesus that figure in the Gospels of Matthew and Luke. As we shall see, neither of them is absolutely straightforward—Matthew's is more exciting than that of Luke—and both have a hidden agenda to pursue.

MATTHEW'S GENEALOGY

As in many other aspects of their recounting of the story of the
Nativity, Matthew and Luke follow different paths in their
presentation of the pedigree of Jesus. The genealogical table
constitutes the opening section of Matthew (Mt 1:1–17),
whereas the parallel material in Luke is placed outside the birth
narrative and is linked to the account of the baptism of Jesus
by John (Lk 3:23–38). As we shall see, the two genealogies also
proceed in opposite directions.

Mt 1:1–6
*The book of the genealogy of Jesus, the son of David, the son of
Abraham. Abraham was the father of Isaac, and Isaac the fa-
ther of Jacob, and Jacob the father of Judah and his brothers, and
Judah the father of Perez by* **Tamar,** *and Perez the father of
Hezron, and Hezron the father of Ram, and Ram the father of
Amminadab, and Amminadab the father of Nahshon, and
Nahshon the father of Salmon, and Salmon the father of Boaz by*
Rahab, *and Boaz the father of Obed by* **Ruth,** *and Obed the fa-
ther of Jesse, and Jesse the father of David the king. And David
was the father of Solomon by* **the wife of Uriah.**

Matthew deliberately imitates the Old Testament when he
chooses for the title of his Gospel the familiar biblical heading
"The Book of the generations." His model is the biblical
Genesis, where the same formula, "Book of generations," introduces the first family tree of mankind, running from Adam to

the sons of Noah, from the creation to the flood (Gen 5:1–32). Matthew at once confronts his readers with two key figures of Jewish history, Abraham, the ancestor of Israel, the father of God's chosen people, and David, the founder of the royal dynasty of Israel, and the forefather of the final ruler, the Messiah. Jesus is characterized straight from the start as Son of Abraham and Son of David, but the main emphasis seems to lie on the second title.

Whilst pretending to offer a direct proof of Jesus' Davidic descent, Matthew's list is far from simple; indeed it is highly artificial. He arranges it so that the ancestors fall for no obvious reason into three periods of fourteen generations. No one so far has come up with a satisfactory explanation for this 3×14. Fourteen has no known significance in Jewish thought apart from being the double of the mystical number seven. It has been suggested that 3×14, being equal to 6×7, would indicate that with Jesus the final seventh period of seven generations would begin, but all this sounds labored and unconvincing. Why would Matthew choose 14 as his basic unit and not the usual figure of 7?

So if Matthew is to be believed, forty-two generations separate Jesus from Abraham and twenty-eight from David. A preliminary glance at the genealogy of Jesus in Luke reveals striking differences. Matthew's register is considerably shorter even for the period covered by both of them, without taking into account the prehistory added by Luke, which extends far beyond Abraham. Did Matthew artificially shorten the third period in order to reduce it to fourteen generations?

The opening section of the genealogy generally mirrors the

Hebrew Bible, but it departs from normal Jewish practice in one important respect: it includes the names of four women. The fifth name, Mary mother of Jesus, will appear in the final generation in the last set of fourteen. This is a remarkable oddity, as biblical genealogy always runs on the paternal line. As far as royal succession is concerned, we read in the Book of Ecclesiasticus, or Wisdom of Ben Sira, one of the Apocrypha dating to the beginning of the second century BC: "The heritage of the king is from son to son only" (Ecclus 45:25). A similar rule governs the inheritance of property too. Matthew's reference to women is patently not regular—there are only four, not fourteen, names of females in the first fourteen generations—nor is it accidental. It has an unspecified message to convey. If we discount Mary, who has a very particular role to play, what the other women mentioned have in common is that they all seem to be of foreign stock or have a foreign husband.

Let us look first at the problem of intermarriage with non-Jewish women among the forebears of Jesus. In the patriarchal age the descendants of Jacob, no doubt to avoid inbreeding, chose wives for themselves and their sons from among the daughters of the inhabitants of the country. Judah, who is on Matthew's list, married a Canaanite girl by the name of Shua (Gen 38:2), and Tamar, the wife of his son Er, was also a Canaanite. After she had lost her husband and Judah had refused to marry her to his last surviving son, employing a stratagem she made herself pregnant by Judah and bore him twin sons. Another Canaanite woman, Rahab, also on Matthew's list, was married to one of Joshua's men, Salmon. The latter's son, Boaz, took for wife a Moabite woman, Ruth, who became the great-grandmother of David (Ruth 4:13–22). The fourth person listed in the female ancestry of Jesus was Bathsheba, whom King David acquired as wife after ordering the commander of his army to ensure that Bathsheba's Hittite husband, Uriah, would not return alive from the battlefield.

The other distinguishing feature of three out of the four women concerned is some kind of marital irregularity. Tamar, the widowed daughter-in-law of Judah, pretended to be a prostitute on the roadside and seduced her father-in-law, who had sex with her without realizing who she was. Rahab was a professional prostitute from Jericho, and Bathsheba committed adultery with David. However, the first two women are held blameless by the Bible and Jewish tradition. In Tamar's case, the guilt lay with Judah, who prevented another of his sons from marrying Tamar. In a rather unusual way she just reasserted her right to bear a son in the family. Rahab redeemed herself when she saved the life of the spies sent by Joshua to reconnoiter the land of Canaan (Josh 6:25). As for the case of Bathsheba, the real culpability lay with David, who not only slept with another man's wife but to all intents and purposes murdered the husband. The Moabite Ruth was guiltless.

When all these considerations are taken into account, the most likely reason for Matthew to single out these women and record their names in the ancestry of the Messiah is his intention to underline that, although Jesus, the son of Abraham, was Jewish, his remote lineage comprised non-Jews too, at least on the female side, and that in consequence he was of interest to non-Jews also. Here is the first surprise disclosure in a genealogical list which is normally regarded as dull. A bigger one is to follow.

Mᴛ 1:7–16

*And Solomon was the father of Rehoboam. And Rehoboam the father of Abijah, and Abijah the father of Asa, and Asa the father of Jehoshaphat, and Jehoshaphat the father of Joram, and Joram the father of Uzziah, and Uzziah the father of Jotham, and Jotham the father of Ahaz, and Ahaz the father of Hezekiah, and Hezekiah the father of Manasseh, and Manasseh the father of Amos, and Amos the father of Josiah, and Josiah the father of Jechoniah and his brothers, at the time of the deportation to Babylon. And after the deportation to Babylon: Jechoniah was the father of Shealtiel, and Shealtiel the father of Zerubbabel, and Zerubbabel the father of Abiud, and Abiud the father of Eliakim, and Eliakim the father of Azor, and Azor the father of Zadok, and Zadok the father of Achim, and Achim the father of Eliud, and Eliud the father of Eleazar, and Eleazar the father of Matthan, and Matthan the father of Jacob, and Jacob the father of Joseph the husband of **Mary**, of whom Jesus **was born,** who is called Christ.*

From Solomon to Jechoniah, a variant of Jehoiachin (see Jer 27:20 as against 2 Kings 24:6), Matthew more or less rigorously excerpts the Books of Kings in the Bible and lists the royal descendants of David. Luke, as will appear, follows a totally different path. With Jechoniah's grandson Zerubbabel, the princely leader who brought back a group of Jews from Babylonia to Judaea in 538 ʙᴄ, the evangelist reaches the end of the Old Testament record serving as the source for his genealogy. From then on, both Matthew and Luke depend on documents unattested in, and partly contradicted by, Scripture. For instance, the son of Zerubbabel in Matthew's genealogy of

Jesus is Abiud, while in Luke the corresponding forefather is called Rhesa. However, one of the Old Testament books has preserved a detailed record of Zerubbabel's descendants, giving the names of no less than seven of his sons: Meshullam, Hananiah, Hashubah, Ohel, Berechiah, Hasadiah, and Jushab-hesed (1 Chr 3:19–20), yet neither Abiud nor Rhesa figures among them. The other individuals down to Jacob, the father of Joseph, that is, the grandfather of Jesus, are totally unknown entities, and as will be shown with possibly one exception they all differ from the corresponding ancestors in Luke's family tree. Short of being held to be entirely fictitious, the names must have been borrowed from traditions relating to the genealogical table of the house of David, unknown in the Bible, in Josephus or in rabbinic literature (see pp. 34–36).

Throughout the whole series, the same formula, "A was the father of B," literally, A "begot" or "procreated" B, is employed as befits a Jewish genealogical record always listing fathers and sons. But when Matthew arrives at Mary, the fifth woman on his list, although without hesitation he still calls Joseph her husband (*anêr*), he modifies the standard pattern "A begot B, B begot C," etc., and changes the linking expression from the active "begot" to the passive "was begotten" or "was born," from the Greek *egennêsen* to *egennêthê*. Clearly the evangelist has a message to pass on. He is determined to avoid an expression which would indicate that Jesus was the normal child of Joseph in a genealogy whose aim is to prove that Jesus descended from David *through Joseph*.

The fluctuating textual tradition reveals that something unusual is afoot here. Significant variations in the Greek codices and in some of the ancient translations of the passage in

Matthew indicate that already in the early centuries of Christianity the copyists and interpreters of this verse were aware of problems and difficulties arising from Matthew 1:16. The hesitations they display indicate the pains the copyists have taken to come up with a suitable formula.

The majority of the Greek manuscripts contain the awk-ward text that has just been quoted: "and Jacob [[was]] the fa-ther of Joseph, the husband of Mary, of whom Jesus *was born* [[or *begotten*]], who is called Christ." What the tradition seeks to obfuscate in this case is the identity of the father. It is not explicitly stated that Joseph, the husband of Mary, did not beget Jesus, but neither are we told who did. In other words the idea of the virgin birth which will be developed a few verses further on is anticipated here by stealth.

Nevertheless, this doctrinal revision was not implemented with full success. Other Greek manuscripts and the Old Latin translation of Matthew 1:16 offer a very different message. They insert a reference to Mary, but safeguard the regular wording of the genealogy which implies that the paternity belongs to Joseph. They read, "Joseph to whom the virgin Mary was be-trothed, *begot* Jesus who was called Christ." The same plain-speaking has been preserved also in the Dialogue of Timothy and Aquila, a Greek composition dated to the fifth century: "Joseph *begot* Jesus who was called Christ" (ed. by F. C. Cony-beare in *The Dialogues of Athanasius and Zacchaeus*, 1898).

Of all the textual testimonies that run counter to the tradi-tional orthodox stance, perhaps the most significant is the old-est Semitic witness, an early Syriac version of Matthew. It was found in the library of the monastery of St. Catherine on

Mount Sinai by two learned and adventurous Scottish ladies, Mrs. Agnes Smith Lewis and Mrs. Margaret Dunlop Gibson, and published in 1894. The so-called Sinaitic Syriac, or syr^{syn}, characteristically preserves even in connection with Jesus the formula which runs through the whole genealogy: "Joseph to whom was betrothed the virgin Mary, *begot* Jesus." But this is not a one-off accident. Five verses later, in Matthew 1:21, the same Syriac version characteristically supplements the words of the angel addressed to Joseph, "she [Mary] will bear a son," by adding "she will bear a son *for you*," which is a commonly used expression to denote paternity. Both passages concur in making crystal clear who the father is meant to be and reveal-ing what must have been the Semitic original subjacent to Matthew 1:16.

The first surprise in Matthew's family tree was the inclu-sion of women; the second is the compelling case for a geneal-ogy of Jesus transmitted in Jewish-Christian circles in Hebrew or Aramaic, in which just as Joseph is the son of Jacob, Jesus is said to have been "begotten" by Joseph. Note also that there is no mention of the virginity of Mary in the main tradition and the same silence on Mary characterizes the family tree sup-plied by Luke too. Jesus is portrayed in Matthew's genealogy as the rightful heir of David, being the son of Joseph, scion of the royal house of Israel. The same position is confirmed, as will be shown in chapter 5, by the doctrine embraced by the Ebionites, a Judeo-Christian community which survived well into the third/fourth century as reported by Church Fathers.

The issue of the paternity of Joseph will be discussed in full detail apropos of the virginal conception of Mary (pp. 53–72).

Mᴛ 1:17

*So all the generations from Abraham to David were fourteen
generations, and from David to the deportation to Babylon fourteen generations, and from the deportation to Babylon to Christ
fourteen generations.*

Matthew had to manipulate his list to arrive at a symmetrical
periodization of three times fourteen units. The last fourteen
generations take us in the post-exilic era of biblical history from
Shealtiel, the son of Jechoniah and the father of Zerubbabel,
through a line of otherwise unknown individuals to Joseph
and to Jesus. But here Matthew, notwithstanding his claim of
fourteen generations, supplies only thirteen names: Shealtiel,
Zerubbabel, Abiud, Eliakim, Azor, Zadok, Achim, Eliud,
Eleazar, Matthan, Jacob, Joseph, Jesus. Has one generation
been accidentally dropped by later scribes? If so, it is amazing
that no subsequent copyist has tried to remedy the error. Was
perhaps the authority of Matthew's textual tradition so great
that people turned a blind eye on his apparent lack of elemen-
tary arithmetical skill? Or did the ancients realize that in a
genre like the Infancy Gospels literal correctness comes second
to other, higher purposes?

LUKE'S GENEALOGY

The first impression we gain when we compare the often dis-
crepant names advanced by Luke with the list of Matthew is
that the documents before us are unlikely to be reliable from
the point of view of history. As has been pointed out, Luke's

genealogy of Jesus is longer than Matthew's. The two coincide only between Abraham and David, where both evangelists directly rely on the information contained in the Hebrew Bible from Genesis to the Books of Kings and Chronicles. However, Luke's genealogy is found outside his Infancy Gospel, and contrary to Matthew's it follows an ascending direction starting with Jesus and continues the line, following biblical precedents, beyond Abraham up to Adam, the father of mankind.

Lk 3:23–38

*Jesus . . . was . . . the son (**as was supposed**) of Joseph, the son of Heli, the son of Matthat [Matthan in Mt], the son of Levi, the son of Melchi, the son of Jannai, the son of Joseph, the son of Mattathias, the son of Amos, the son of Nahum, the son of Esli, the son of Naggai, the son of Maath, the son of Mattathias, the son of Semein, the son of Josech, the son of Joda, the son of Joanan, the son of Rhesa, the son of Zerubbabel, the son of Shealtiel, the son of Neri, the son of Melchi, the son of Addi, the son of Cosam, the son of Elmadam, the son of Er, the son of Joshua, the son of Eliezer, the son of Jorim, the son of Matthat, the son of Levi, the son of Simeon, the son of Judah, the son of Joseph, the son of Jonam, the son of Eliakim, the son of Melea, the son of Menna, the son of Mattatha, the son of Nathan, the son of David, the son of Jesse, the son of Obed, the son of Boaz, the son of Sala [Salmon in Mt], the son of Nahshon, the son of Amminadab, the son of Admin, the son of Arni, the son of Hezron, the son of Perez, the son of Judah, the son of Jacob, the son of Isaac, the son of Abraham, the son of Terah, the son of Nahor, the son of Serug, the son of Reu, the son of Peleg, the son of Eber, the son of Shelah, the son of Cainan, the son of*

Arphaxad, the son of Shem, the son of Noah, the son of Lamech, the son of Methuselah, the son of Enoch, the son of Jared, the son of Mahalaleel, the son of Cainan, the son of Enos, the son of Seth, the son of Adam, the son of God.

In order to make possible a comparison between the lists of Matthew and Luke, the order of the names in Luke will be reversed to begin with God and Adam and finish with Joseph and Jesus.

Matthew	Luke
	God
	Adam
	Seth
	Enos
	Cainan
	Mahalaleel
	Jared
	Enoch
	Methuselah
	Lamech
	Noah
	Shem
	Arphaxad
	Cainan
	Shelah
	Eber
	Peleg

	Reu
	Serug
	Nahor
	Terah
Abraham	Abraham
Isaac	Isaac
Jacob	Jacob
Judah [by *Tamar*]	Judah
Perez	Perez
Hezron	Hezron
Aram	Arni [?Aram]
	Admin
Amminadab	Amminadab
Nahshon	Nahshon
Salmon [by *Rahab*]	Sala
Boaz [by *Ruth*]	Boaz
Obed	Obed
Jesse	Jesse
David [by the *wife of Uriah*]	David
Solomon	Nathan
Rehoboam	Mattatha
Abijah	Menna
Asaph	Melea
Jehoshaphat	Jonam
	Joseph
	Judah
	Simeon
Joram	Levi
Uzziah	Matthat

	Jotham	Jorim
	Ahaz	Eliezer
	Hezekiah	Joshua
	Manasseh	Er
	Amos	Elmadam
	Josiah	Cosam
		Addi
		Melchi
	Jechoniah	Neri
Shealtiel	**Shealtiel**	
	Zerubbabel	**Zerubbabel**
	Abiud	Rhesa
		Joanan
		Joda
		Josech
		Semein
	Eliakim	Mattathias
	Azor	Maath
		Naggai
	Zadok	Esli
		Nahum
	Achim	Amos
	Eliud	Mattathias
		Joseph
	Eleazar	Jannai
		Melchi
		Levi
	Matthan	Matthat ⟦?**Matthan**⟧
	Jacob	Heli

Joseph [husband of *Mary*]   **Joseph** [*supposed* father]
          Jesus   **Jesus**

A few comments are apposite for the explanation of the two
parallel lists. Only the names printed in bold characters are
common to both Infancy Gospels. Compared to Matthew,
Luke's genealogy is fuller but is also more straightforward.
Starting with Jesus, he traces back his line in seventy-seven
stages, a multiple of the mystic number 7, to the first man,
Adam. Jesus is forty-two generations away from King David
(not twenty-eight as in Matthew), and another fourteen generations take him back to Abraham. Between Shealtiel and Jesus
twenty-two names are given in Luke against Matthew's thirteen. If we keep Joseph out of the count, the only common
ancestor of Jesus in both lists (other than Shealtiel and
Zerubbabel) is Matthan, provided that Luke's corresponding
name Matthat is considered as a mere scribal variant. But he
could just as well be a different person.

On the whole, we seem to be faced in Luke with a less
stereotyped, normal genealogy. In Matthew, only the name of
Jacob is repeated; in Luke we find Joseph three times, Matthat
twice, Mattatha and Mattathias once each, but it is not impossible that the last three names, designating four persons, are ultimately one and the same (Mattathias). It is furthermore
significant to observe that no woman is mentioned, not even
Mary. The sole departure from a straight list of sons and fathers concerns Luke's qualification that Joseph was the "*supposed*" father of Jesus. But this insertion is patently secondary
and parenthetic. Its aim is to make the genealogy conform to
the earlier story of the virginal conception and explain away

the conflict with the paternal quality of Joseph (Lk 1:26–38; see also chapter 5).

The royal descent is only implicitly asserted insofar as David is given as one of Jesus' many forefathers. Curiously, the line of succession is traced not through Solomon and the Jewish kings as in Matthew, but through Nathan, another son of David, whose descendants did not sit on the royal throne. In fact, none of them is mentioned in the Old Testament. However, no specific importance should be attached to the absence of emphasis on royal extraction since earlier Luke has already twice characterized Joseph as a member of the house of David (Lk 1:27; 2:4). Nevertheless, the diminished stress on the Davidic connection may insinuate that, for Luke, Jesus is more than an heir to royalty. He has previously called him "*the Son of the Most High*" (Lk 1:32) and he is in the last resort the counterpart of Adam, also designated as "*the son of God.*" If, as is usually thought, Luke was a disciple of Paul, the ending of Luke's genealogy would echo the Pauline doctrine of the two Adams—the first and the last, the father of mankind and Christ—in 1 Corinthians 15:45–49.

A final remark on the two genealogies. The substantial differences between Matthew and Luke are beyond dispute and have always puzzled the theologians and the Bible interpreters of the Church. New Testament scholars have attempted since time immemorial to iron out the discrepancies and reconcile them, but without visible success. We encounter the first major effort to solve the dilemma as far back as the early third century. It is attached to the name of Julius Africanus, a learned Palestinian Christian. In his opinion the contradictions between the lists of Matthew and Luke must stem from the

Jewish law concerning leviratic marriage. Leviratic, or brother-in-law, marriage entails the moral obligation of a brother to marry his deceased brother's childless widow. The first male issue of the new union becomes by legal fiction the heir of the dead brother, so that his line would continue and his property would remain undivided. If so, Julius Africanus must have surmised, the disagreements between the two genealogical tables arose from one evangelist recording the name of the biological father and the other that of the legal one. At closer inspection, however, this apparently clever idea turns out to be a failure. It could no doubt account for occasional diversity, but it is unsuitable as an explanation for two lists which disagree with one another so fundamentally and on so many points. In fact, between David and Joseph the two genealogies propose only two, or at best three, names (Shealtiel, Zerubbabel, and Matthan/Matthat) that are the same! Other theories accept that complete harmonization is impossible and opt therefore for an entirely new solution. The two lists vary because we are faced with the genealogies of two different persons, namely, the two parents. Matthew gives Joseph's family tree and Luke Mary's. But this theory is totally unfounded, as there is no hint whatever in Luke that he is dealing with Mary. In fact, not even her name appears anywhere on the list of ancestors. Besides, what possible purpose could a maternal genealogy serve in a Jewish setting?

Unless we assume the not impossible theory that both evangelists largely shaped their documents themselves—this would not be the only well-meant act of creativity (*pia fraus*) in religious history—the most probable explanation of the enigma is that the aim pursued by Matthew and Luke in compiling their genealogies was doctrinal, and not historical. To prove the Davidic family connection of Jesus, a prerequisite of his Messianic standing, they probably employed documents. But since their records are contradictory, they must have laid their hands on separate registers of David's descendants. All they needed to do was to re-edit them so that they both ended (or started) with Joseph and Jesus (or Jesus and Joseph). This was definitely possible, as we know from Jewish as well as from Christian sources that genealogical lists of this sort were circulating among the Jewish inhabitants of Palestine at the beginning of the Christian era.

Let us start with Jewish parallels. Among these, particular attention must be drawn to rabbinic documents that refer to the Scroll of Pedigree, or Megillat Yohasin, a written family record which was, we are told, found in Jerusalem purportedly in the first century AD. Its importance lies in the assertion that the famous teacher Hillel the Elder, an older contemporary of Jesus, was a direct descendant of King David (yTaanit 68a). Another rabbinic text gives the same statement concerning Hillel's Davidic connection as an illustration of the messianic prophecy "The scepter shall not depart from Judah" in Gen 49:10 (Genesis Rabbah 98:8). Reference to these texts is meant only to imply that a document such as the Scroll of Pedigree actually existed, without taking on board what is asserted in them, namely, Hillel's Davidic ancestry. In fact, we can nowhere find any trace of Hillel himself alleging that he was the Messiah or that anyone else proclaimed him as such. By contrast, we are told that the head of Babylonian Jewry, Rab Huna (c. AD 200) was actually thought to be a member of the Messianic tribe of Judah.

On the Christian side, the second-century writer Hege-sippus, whose work, or at least part of it, has been preserved in the *Ecclesiastical History* of Eusebius (3:20, 1–6), reports that the emperor Domitian (AD 81–96), in his effort to wipe out all the Jewish revolutionary movements, decided to rid Palestine of the last surviving representatives of the family of David. Not surprisingly, these Church historians include in the royal house of David some of the late-first-century relatives of Jesus. Eusebius testifies to the rumor that the grandsons of Jude, the brother of the Lord, that is to say the great-nephews of Jesus, had to suffer as a result of the Roman persecution. However, assuming that the story is true, such a persecution could not have been organized unless the local authorities had possessed evidence on which to institute charges.

Julius Africanus, who has been cited earlier (p. 34), further asserts that as late as the early third century, some of the in-habitants of Nazareth still paraded as "The Master's People" (*Desposunoi*). They claimed that they were relatives of Jesus. What is more, they said they could prove this with "private records" and apparently they "took pride in preserving the memory of their aristocratic origin" (Eusebius, *Ecclesiastical History* 1:7, 14). Julius Africanus had a critical mind and re-mained skeptical of the reliability of these tales. Nevertheless, Eusebius' records indicate that such documents, however inau-thentic, continued to circulate. If that was the case in the third century, it is even more likely that Matthew and Luke at the end of the first century could come across some of them and in-corporate them in their Infancy Gospels as evidence of the Messianic entitlement of Jesus.

In sum, since the Davidic descent is an indispensable factor, the claim that Jesus was the son of Joseph "of the house of David" acquires outstanding importance. However, establishing a justifiable claim to the Messianic title is one thing and the notion of the virginal conception of Jesus quite another. By endeavoring to combine the two, Matthew and Luke unwittingly confused the aim of the genealogies. For if in order to proclaim the virgin birth, they had to deny the real paternity of Joseph, they were unavoidably bound to undermine the royal Messianic claim of Jesus.

| 4 |

The Idea of Miraculous Births in
Judaism and Paganism

❧❦❧

O N THE ESSENTIAL TOPICS OF THE
Nativity tale both Matthew and Luke
concur. God's Holy Spirit is said to
have played an essential, though ill-defined,
part in Mary's pregnancy and brought about
what is termed in traditional Christian parlance a virginal conception. This doctrine of the
virginal conception and birth of Jesus forms an
essential part of the teaching of the Church
and on a more popular level of the Christmas
story: Mary became pregnant and gave birth to
a son without ceasing to be a virgin and without the participation of a man in the process of
impregnation. This dogma is exclusively based
on a few verses of the Infancy Gospels; no
other section of the New Testament inside or

outside the Gospels makes any reference to it either explicitly or even implicitly.

Though such a virginal conception is unparalleled in the Hebrew Bible or in postbiblical Jewish literature in antiquity, stories implying some kind of miraculous birth circulated in abundance in the various corners of the ancient world, both among Jews and among pagans. It is necessary, therefore, to form an idea of the cultural background that conditioned the thinking of the writers and the readership of the New Testament before tackling the Gospel accounts themselves.

To grasp the import of the imagery associated with miraculous births, we must bear in mind that in the age and in the civilization of Jesus the knowledge of physiology was fairly rudimentary and the mystery of fertility was steeped in religious awe. In pagan antiquity fruitfulness was thought to depend on special gods or goddesses, and in biblical Judaism on the one God of Israel. According to the colorful language of the Hebrew Bible, this God had the power to close the womb or to open it. If he closed it, the woman remained sterile. If he opened the womb, she became fertile. In short, in some sense every pregnancy was seen as mediated by God, as a divine gift, but some more so than others. However, in the Jewish view, even a miraculous, i.e., heavenly assisted, conception presupposed prior sexual intercourse. The spouses were expected to play their part in the process.

EXTRAORDINARY BIRTH STORIES
IN THE OLD TESTAMENT

To begin with, Jesus' birth should be considered against the "miraculous" or quasi-miraculous pregnancies reported in a number of Old Testament narratives. The women in question are all depicted as barren, having suffered sterility for a long time, and in several instances they are elderly matrons far beyond the childbearing age. The wives of several of the Hebrew Patriarchs are reported to have been infertile for substantial periods. Sarah, the spouse of Abraham, was still childless when she reached the age of ninety. She is expressly described as having passed the menopause—"it had ceased to be with her after the manner of women" (Gen 18:11)—and to crown her handicaps, in the person of Abraham she had a centenarian for a husband: "After I have grown old, and my husband is old, shall I have pleasure?" (Gen 18:12). Nevertheless, by virtue of a divine promise Sarah was enabled to give birth to Isaac (Gen 21:1). Isaac's wife, Rebekah, was also barren, but Isaac's persistent prayer made God intervene and the twins Esau and Jacob were "miraculously" born (Gen 25:21–24). Jacob's hopes of posterity were equally frustrated for a long while and both his wives, Leah and Rachel, remained childless. But God took pity first on Leah, the unloved wife, and "opened her womb," while her sister Rachel, Jacob's favorite, continued to be without progeny. Exasperated, Rachel tried to blame her condition on Jacob, but he angrily reminded her that barrenness was a woman's failure and that ultimately pregnancy was a divine gift: "Am I in the place of God, who has withheld from you the fruit of the womb?" Later, in answer to Rachel's supplication, God "remembered her and opened her womb," and the much beloved Patriarch Joseph was born (Gen 29:31; 30:2, 22–23). Likewise Hannah, the mother of the prophet Samuel, was unimpressed by the words of Elkanah, her male chauvinist of a husband, "Am I not more to you than ten sons?," until her prayers, repeated year in, year out, induced God to act and give her a male offspring (1 Sam 1:1–20).

In Luke's infancy narrative the tale of the pregnancy of Elizabeth, the mother of John the Baptist (Lk 1:7, 11–13, 18–20, 57), is modeled on the Samuel anecdote just cited. It is recounted in preparation of the story of the miraculous birth of Jesus. But while the dominant idea of divine participation in procuring pregnancy helps the understanding of the unusual conception of Jesus, the standard biblical solution of female infertility, the removal of long-term sterility through direct action of God, cannot be applied in Mary's case, as she was young and unmarried. Nevertheless, as we shall see (pp. 69–70), youth itself may hold the key to an unforeseen solution to the problem.

"SONS OF GOD" AND "DAUGHTERS OF MEN"

The Old Testament and Jewish literature of the inter-Testamental age furnish an alternative opening. It consists of legends about progeny born out of the union of heavenly beings or angels and terrestrial women. For the sophisticated readers of our age, such tales may look exceedingly silly and fanciful, but the Infancy Gospels were composed almost two millennia ago for people steeped in speculations of this sort. Weird birth stories, not unlike age-old oriental and Graeco-Roman myths, circulated among Jews in New Testament times, and the Jewish and Gentile public, addressed by the Infancy Gospels both in Palestine and in the Diaspora, was familiar with them. The starting point of the Jewish fables is the biblical Book of Genesis, which has preserved the amazing tale of the "sons of God." They fell for the charms of the "daughters of men," and, captivated by their beauty, they abandoned their comfortable heavenly abode and came down to earth bodily to enjoy female company. As one might guess, the adventure quickly went awry. Their offspring turned out to be giants whose depravity brought on Noah's flood and almost completely destroyed mankind (Gen 6:1–4).

By "sons of God" the Jews of the age of Jesus understood angels, as we learn from the Greek Septuagint translation of the Bible, the Book of Jubilees, a version of Genesis rewritten in the second century BC, the Dead Sea Scrolls, and other ancient Jewish works. The misconduct of these heavenly "playboys" is described with gusto in the First Book of Enoch (third/second century BC) and in later rabbinic literature. They initiated their girlfriends in the use of all kinds of cosmetics, in particular in "the art of making up the eyes," and as a result fornication entered the world. They also taught them spells, incantations, and all kinds of wizardry (1 Enoch 8).

But Jewish thought did not restrict the attractiveness of female beauty to angels of the pre-diluvian age. A second-century BC version of the ordeals of the Patriarch Lamech can be read in the Genesis Apocryphon from Qumran, an Aramaic paraphrase of Genesis. At the sight of the brilliant light that filled the house and surrounded the baby Noah, Lamech began to wonder whether the child produced by Bathenosh was not really the son of an angel with whom his wife had consorted. Lamech's suspicion was soon dispelled by the firm protest of Bathenosh: "I swear to you by the Holy Great One"—his furious wife expostulated—"that this seed is yours and that [this] conception is from you. This fruit was planted by you ... and by no stranger, or Watcher, or Son of Heaven" (Gen Apocryphon 2). The bright light, which according to the story radiated from and around Noah, suggests that in the view of the Jews of that age the offspring of an angel and a woman was not necessarily evil. In the Bible and in postbiblical Judaism, light always had positive associations.

The idea of potential sexual rapport between angels and women continued to float in the air even as late as in New Testament times. Indeed, when St. Paul forbade the female members of the church of Corinth to attend Christian assemblies with the head uncovered, he justified this prohibition by his belief that the sight of their hair might lead astray some passing-by sons of heaven: "That is why a woman ought to have a veil on her head, *because of the angels*," Paul insisted (1 Cor 11:10). The influence of this legend on early Christian thought is attested by the author of the Protoevangelium of James, a New Testament apocryphon dating to the second half of the second century, which is full of popular speculation about Joseph, Mary, and the child Jesus. According to Pseudo-James, when Mary was questioned by Joseph about her pregnancy, she protested under oath that she had no idea how it came about. (In this story there is no allusion to the annunciation by Gabriel.) It is not surprising in the circumstances that the first thought crossing Joseph's mind was that she was carrying the seed of an angel (Protoevangelium 13:2–14:1). The idea is clearly odd, but it is not unprecedented.

THE METAPHOR OF GOD "BEGETTING" HUMANS

Matthew and Luke expressly call Mary's baby "the Son of God." In Matthew the designation is derived from biblical prophecy seen as fulfilled in Jesus. In Isaiah 7 the son conceived by the virgin is called Emmanuel, or "God with us," and his return from Egypt realizes the words placed on the lips of the Lord by the prophet Hosea, "Out of Egypt have I called *my son*" (Hosea 11:1 in Mt 2:15). In Luke the angel Gabriel directly and explicitly announces the birth of "the Son of the Most High" and "the Son of God" (Lk 1:32, 35).

It is common knowledge that before the New Testament, the Hebrew Bible and the Dead Sea Scrolls regularly speak of "sons of God" and occasionally refer to God in figurative speech as "begetting" or "procreating" a human being. In the Bible and in writings produced during the centuries that followed the completion of the Old Testament, "Son of God" occurs in a variety of meanings. In addition to the angels already discussed, among the humans "Son of God" was the title of anyone believed in some way to be linked to God. Every male Israelite could pride himself on being a "son of God," and reciprocally he was in a position to call God his Father. In the course of time, the phrase was also applied—more and more restrictively—to the good Jews, to the especially holy Jews, culminating with the king of the Jews and finally with the Messiah, the most holy and powerful future ruler of Israel about whom we read in the Florilegium, one of the Dead Sea Scrolls, "I will be his Father and he shall be my Son. He is the Branch of David" (see my *Jesus the Jew*, pp. 168–73).

The Jewish king, while the monarchy existed down to 586 BC, and the awaited royal Messiah after the Babylonian exile were symbolically portrayed as *engendered* by the Deity: "You are my son, today *I have begotten you*," we read in Psalm 2:7. The Rule of the Congregation among the Dead Sea Scrolls also speaks of God "begetting" the Messiah (1 QSerekh a 2:11–12). The phrase in the Qumran Aramaic Apocalypse, "The Son of God he will be proclaimed, and the Son of the Most High they will call him" (4Q246, 2:1), whatever its precise meaning may be, is curiously reminiscent of Luke 1:32, 35 (see pp. 66–67).

It is universally agreed among experts that in Judaism the phrase is always used metaphorically; it never designates a person who is believed to be simultaneously man and God, a human being who also shares in some way divine nature. In this respect, from the monotheistic point of view, the Jewish inhabitants of the Holy Land found themselves in a privileged position compared to those Jews and Gentiles who lived outside Palestine, in countries imbued with Graeco-Roman religious culture, full of legends about the miraculous, divinely effected birth of heroes and great leaders, past and present.

MIRACULOUS BIRTHS IN THE PAGAN WORLD

Leaving aside classic Graeco-Roman mythology, with half-divine, half-human offspring resulting, for example, from the amorous escapades of Zeus, fathering Heracles, Dionysus, Castor and Pollux, and Perseus out of Alcmene, Semele, Leda, and Danae, we also encounter numerous allusions to the super-human origin of historical personalities in ancient Greek and Latin literature. Let us ignore stories relating to early Roman history, such as Romulus having Mars as his father (Ovid, *Metamorphoses*, 14:805–28), and concentrate on figures closer to Jesus' time who had the reputation of being fathered by a god.

The first of these to mention is Plato, that giant among Greek philosophers, who was believed to be "not the son of Ariston, but of a visionary figure who came to Amphictione (Plato's mother) in the form of Apollo" (Origen quoting Celsus in *Against Celsus* 6:8). The legend repeated by Celsus further asserts that before Plato was born, "Ariston [his father] was prevented from having sexual intercourse with Amphictione until she had brought forth the child which she had by Apollo" (Origen, ibid. 1:37)—a curious parallel to Matthew's remark concerning Joseph not "knowing" Mary while she had Jesus in her womb (Mt 1:25, see p. 55).

As one might have guessed, Alexander the Great was also credited with divine origin. Olympias, his mother, is said to have been impregnated not by her husband, Philip, king of Macedon, who was apparently afraid of sharing her bed because of her habit of sleeping with snakes, but by Zeus

(Plutarch, *Life of Alexander* 3:1, 3). Earlier Plutarch remarked that Philip "shrank from her embraces in the conviction that she was the partner of a superior being" (ibid. 2:2, 3).

In connection with the emperor Augustus, who ruled the world at the time of the birth of Jesus, Asclepiades of Mendes recounts in his book entitled *Theologoumena* that Atia, Augustus' mother, once attended in the company of certain married women friends a solemn midnight service at the Temple of Apollo, where she had her litter set down, and presently fell asleep: "Suddenly a serpent glided up, entered her and then glided away again. On awakening, she purified herself, as if after intimacy with her husband . . . The birth of Augustus nine months later suggested a divine paternity" (Suetonius, *Augustus* 94). The divinity of Augustus was derived both from this tale and from his family link with Julius Caesar. He was honored as *Divi Filius*, or the deified Caesar's son.

It is impossible to establish with any degree of certainty how much the apotheosis of great historical figures in the Graeco-Roman world subconsciously influenced the thinking of Gentile converts to Christianity or even deeply Hellenized Jews in the first and second centuries, but the case of Julius Caesar is worth bearing in mind. The elevation of Caesar to divine status cannot be traced to his birth, but occurred about the end of his lifetime and was completed soon after his death. Shortly before his assassination in 44 BC, he permitted the erection of a statue to himself with the inscription *deo invicto* ("to the Unvanquished God"). "His immediate deification"—Suetonius tells us—"was more than a mere official decree since it reflected public conviction" (*Divus Iulius* 88). Indeed in

January 42 BC, less than two years after the fatal Ides of March, the Senate inscribed Caesar among the gods of the Roman state, and in 29 BC a temple was erected in his honor on the Forum (Dio, *Roman History* 47:18, 3). It is bizarre to note, but still worthy of consideration, that the sophisticated sena- tors of Rome needed considerably less time to deify Caesar than the supposedly credulous and simple first Gentile Christians required for acknowledging Jesus as God. None- theless, the elevation of a human being to divine status was un- doubtedly easier for non-Jews than it was for their Jewish contemporaries.

A word needs to be said about the first-century AD Cappadocian Apollonius of Tyana, a Pythagorean sage, often compared to Jesus. He was held by the ordinary folk of his own age to be the son of Zeus (Philostratus, *Apollonius of Tyana* 1:6). He was also venerated for his miraculous cures and for raising the dead. Later his pagan admirers in their anti- Christian polemics extolled him as a figure greater than Christ.

Finally, we must mention in passing the strange legend, popular in the region of the "rose-red" desert city of Petra and possibly also in Southern Palestine. It concerns the Nabataean deity Dusares. The Church Father Epiphanius, a native Palestinian who became bishop of Salamis in Cyprus in the fourth century, narrates that on the feast of this god, which like Christmas fell on December 25, hymns were sung to him and to his mother, Kkhbou. Dusares was celebrated, in curious resemblance of Christian ideas, as "Alone-begotten [*mono- genês*] of the Lord" and in Arabic his mother was called *Chaamou*, that is, "the Virgin" (*Panarion* 51).

No doubt an attempt to explain the virginal conception of

Jesus exclusively by means of these pagan stories would be found convincing only by those who are already that way inclined. Nevertheless, these legends are helpful for reconstructing the mentality of the Gentiles who were targeted by the writers of the Gospels, as well as for grasping the turn of mind of those Hellenized Jews who, like Philo, were thoroughly immersed in classical culture and religion.

HELLENISTIC JEWISH BIRTH STORIES IN PHILO

While the extramarital affairs of the Olympian gods were nothing out of the ordinary in the context of classical mythology, a similar easygoing behavior could hardly be contemplated in connection with the God of Israel, not even in Hellenistic Jewish circles accustomed to pagan myths. Nevertheless, an analogous imagery, used in a strictly symbolical context, found its way into the writings of the Alexandrian Jewish philosopher Philo (c. 20 BC–c. AD 50). He has the habit of comparing the virtues and the fruit they produce with the help of divine power to women and their children, and occasionally this comparison leads him to strikingly imaginative and innovative allegorization.

For instance, when he speculates about Sarah, the ninety-year-old matriarch, he notices that according to the Bible she conceived Isaac when she was alone with God, and Abraham was absent from the scene (see Gen 21:1). From this, Philo deduces that Sarah owed her pregnancy and the birth of Isaac to God, who was "the Author of her visitation" (*The Cherubim*

45). In other words, Isaac was *begotten* by God, and since the name Isaac derives from the verb "to laugh," Philo characterizes him as "the laughter of the heart, *a son of God*" (*The Change of Names* 131). Elsewhere he goes even further in his figurative treatment of the subject: "When Happiness [[= Isaac]] has been born, Sarah says with pride, 'The Lord has made laughter for me ...' (Gen 21:6). Therefore ... open your ears wide ..., writes Philo. The *laughter* [[= Isaac]] is joy, and *has made* is equivalent to 'beget', so that what is said is ... *The Lord begat Isaac* ..." (*The Allegory of the Laws* 218–19). In short, Sarah conceived of God and gave birth to the Son of God.

Quoting another passage of Genesis, which refers to God's opening Leah's womb (Gen 29:31), Philo points out that the Bible attributes to the Deity something that normally "belongs to the husband," namely, impregnation (*The Cherubim* 46). Along the same lines, in connection with Genesis 25:21, Philo recounts that the barren Rebekah became pregnant through the power of God (*The Cherubim* 47), an image that is a straight parallel to Mary's conceiving of the Holy Spirit.

If we bear in mind that in the last resort the Greek story of the virginal conception of Jesus by Mary was transmitted in a Hellenized Jewish and Gentile milieu, we must presume that it had been understood in the meaning to which such a milieu was accustomed.

This summary survey of the thinking of ancient Jews and non-Jews about the supernatural birth of heroes and saints in the age preceding the writing of the infancy narratives of Matthew and Luke will assist the reader in his effort to come to grips with the New Testament message and its complexities dealing with the Virgin and the Holy Spirit.

The Virgin and the Holy Spirit

HE QUINTESSENCE OF MATTHEW'S MES-
sage regarding the miraculous birth
of Jesus is that Mary was "found
with child *of the Holy Spirit*" (Mt 1:18) and
that her offspring was to be called "Emmanuel,"
or "God with us," as predicted in Isaiah's
prophecy (Mt 1:23). Likewise, in Luke the *virgin* called Mary learns that she will conceive
of "*the Holy Spirit*" and be overshadowed by
"*the Power of the Most High.*" As a result, her
"*holy*" child will be "*the Son of God*" (Lk 1:31,
35). Whatever else these mysterious statements
may mean, they certainly describe a child conceived in a way different from the normal and
convey that the person to be born will be very
specially connected with God.

In Matthew's play the lead actor is Joseph.

It is he who learns from an angel appearing in his dream the secret of how Mary has conceived. It is Joseph who has to decide what attitude to take toward her while awaiting the birth of the baby. As far as the geographical setting is concerned, at this stage Bethlehem is the only place mentioned (Mt 2:1). Nazareth is not referred to until the end of Matthew's infancy account.

MATTHEW'S STORY OF JESUS' CONCEPTION

Mt 1:18–25

Now the birth of Jesus Christ took place this way. When his mother Mary had been betrothed to Joseph, before they came together she was found to be with child of the Holy Spirit; and her husband Joseph being a just man and unwilling to put her to shame, resolved to divorce her quietly. But as he considered this, behold, an angel of the Lord appeared to him in a dream, saying, "Joseph, son of David, do not fear to take Mary your wife, for that which is conceived in her is of the Holy Spirit; she will bear a son, and you shall call his name Jesus, for he will save his people from their sins." All this took place to fulfill what the Lord had spoken by the prophet: "Behold, a virgin shall conceive and bear a son, and his name shall be Emmanuel" (which means, God with us). When Joseph woke from sleep, he did as the angel of the Lord commanded him; he took his wife, but knew her not until she had borne a son; and he called his name Jesus.

Matthew's narrative opens with the terse general heading "Now the birth of Jesus Christ took place this way," but nei-

ther here nor in chapter 2 do we learn anything about the
external circumstances in which Jesus was born. Neither the
gist of the genealogy, consisting of a sequence of procreation,
nor the mention that Mary has been engaged to marry Joseph
and thus produce children suggests that in the logic of the
original narration an unparalleled birth was contemplated
which had nothing to do with sex. Indeed, it can be firmly asserted that there is no trace in biblical or postbiblical Jewish
tradition that would anticipate a pregnancy with no male con-
tribution. As has been noted, virginal conception is never contemplated in Judaism, not even in the case of the King Messiah.
What follows here is something unexpected, surprising, and to
a large extent confusing.

The account opens dramatically with Joseph's shock and
dismay in discovering that his fiancée is with child. The Gospel
of Matthew does not identify the place where Mary and
Joseph live, but since there is no question of any change of residence between this moment and the actual birth of Jesus, the
conclusion must be that in Matthew's view the couple always
resided in Bethlehem. The matter of the pregnancy is so dis-
turbing that the evangelist feels obliged in advance to disclose
the reason for it to his readers. They are in the know even before the sleeping Joseph is informed about it by an angelic messenger in his dream. The baffled husband-to-be instinctively
imagines the worst and decides that in the circumstances the
marital agreement must be terminated. However, being a righteous, that is to say, a decent man, he proposes to do so pri-
vately without bringing the case before a law court. In his
dream the following night, he is reassured that Mary's condition is due not to infidelity but to a miraculous intervention by

God. In a scenario reduced to the strict minimum, Joseph at once proceeds to make Mary his wife and thus call an end to the betrothal. However, to ensure that his readers do not draw erroneous conclusions, Matthew informs them that Joseph is going to abstain from cohabiting with Mary as husband and wife until the birth of Jesus (Mt 1:25). Luke, as we shall see, leaves matters unresolved and says nothing on the subject.

Two issues of Jewish law, betrothal and divorce, are implicated in this account, and they require some clarification. To begin with betrothal, in Matthew (as in Luke) Joseph and Mary are said to be engaged. To appreciate properly the meaning of betrothal, it is to be remembered that in the Jewish society of the age of Jesus, arranged marriage was the established custom. The betrothal of a young girl was the prerogative of her father. If the father was no longer alive, his place was taken by the girl's brother or some other male relative. The head of the family negotiated the financial settlement with the groom and his parents. The girl had no say whatever in the matter. Quite apart from the subordinate status of women in Jewish law, in the rabbinic era and no doubt earlier too, the bride-to-be was by definition a *minor*, a person not yet of age. It should be noted that in the Mishnaic-Talmudic legislation, girls attained majority when they started to menstruate, or on the day after their twelfth birthday, whichever came first. In the rabbinic perspective, majority and attainment of puberty were coterminous. By the age of twelve years and six months, a young woman became, in the terminology of the rabbis, "mature" (*bogeret*), and was expected already to be married. In any case, by then her father no longer had the right unilaterally to betroth her.

Once the preliminary requirements laid down in the agreement of betrothal were satisfied, nuptials followed: they were
presumed to take place within twelve months from the date of
engagement. Then the bridegroom led his bride to his own
home amid solemn festivities attended by family, friends, and
neighbors. The Gospels contain various parables about Jewish
weddings (see, for example, Mt 25:1–13). It would follow from
these rules, which appear standard and long-standing, and not
some kind of innovation by the redactors of the Mishnah, that
at the time of the incidents described in the Gospels of
Matthew and Luke, Mary was no more than twelve years old,
or conceivably a little less, and by the standards of her society
and age, mature enough for marriage.

To understand Joseph's dilemma on noticing Mary's pregnancy, we must bear in mind that Jewish betrothal was as
binding as marriage itself and an engaged woman who had sex
with a man other than her fiancé became an adulteress.
According to Matthew's narrative, Joseph realized before the
marriage ceremony had taken place that Mary was expecting a
child, and since he was at once intent on canceling the marital
arrangements, he is patently depicted as a man who did not
consider himself responsible for the pregnancy in question. In
the given circumstances, the engagement could be nullified either in full legal publicity or without too much fuss. In the first
alternative, the young woman would be charged with the
crime of adultery before a tribunal, and if the charge was
proved, she and her paramour would be condemned to death
by stoning. But there was another, less drastic way of terminating the agreement, through issuing a document of repudiation.
Matthew's Joseph opted for a quiet divorce (Mt 1:19). The

concept of such a private dissolution of a marriage by the husband is associated in Jewish writings from the second century BC with two of the biblical Patriarchs. We learn from the Genesis Apocryphon, one of the Dead Sea Scrolls, that should Sarah have actually been forced to sleep with Pharaoh after she had been abducted to the royal harem in Egypt, Abraham would have been obliged to repel her for good (Gen Apocryphon 20:15). Also, the Book of Jubilees relates that Jacob ended cohabitation with Bilhah, his concubine, after she had had sex with his son Reuben even though Bilhah did so innocuously, not realizing that the man in her bed was her stepson Reuben, and not Jacob (Jubilees 33:7–9). In Matthew, Joseph luckily escapes the need to implement his painful decision: the angelic dream vindicates Mary's innocence. He learns that the mysterious impregnation was the work of the Holy Spirit.

The last detail of this part of the story concerns name-giving. Joseph is instructed by the angel to call the child Jesus, accompanied by the explanation of the name—"Jesus" signifying "he will save his people from their sins" (Mt 1:21). Such an explanatory gloss is a well-established Jewish custom since biblical times. For example, Hagar, Abraham's concubine, is ordered to call her son Ishmael ("God hears") "because the Lord has given heed to your affliction" (Gen 16:11).

THE VIRGINAL CONCEPTION IN MATTHEW AND ISAIAH'S PROPHECY

So far, Matthew has told a perplexing story. Apart from alluding to some kind of involvement of the Holy Spirit, a phrase designating the power through which God acts in the world, the angel in the dream offers no elucidation of how Mary has become pregnant. The evangelist steps in, therefore, and sheds new light on the problem with the help of an Old Testament prophecy which predicts that a virgin is to give birth to the Savior of the Jewish people. In the Gospel's version of the words of Isaiah, the prophecy declares: "Behold, a *virgin* shall conceive and bear a son, and his name shall be *Emmanuel* (which means, God with us)" (Isa 7:14 in Mat 1:23).

This is the first biblical proof text produced by Matthew in his infancy narrative. Luke has none. But this prophetic evidence, the purpose of which is to announce a miraculous pregnancy or virginal conception, is effective on one condition: it works only if we follow the Greek Septuagint version of Isaiah 7:14, intended for Greek speakers and understood as Greek readers would understand it. Needless to say, Matthew's Gospel in its extant form is in Greek and as such it was obviously aimed at a Greek audience. However, the original public for which the tradition of the birth narrative of Jesus was developed was Palestinian Jewish and the language in which it was first transmitted was either Aramaic or possibly Hebrew, *not* Greek. Also, it goes without saying that for these Palestinian, mostly Galilean, Jews, the text of Isaiah would have been quoted from the Hebrew Bible, and *not* from the Greek Septuagint.

And this leaves us in a real quandary. To allude to the woman who is going to conceive and bear a son, the Hebrew Isaiah 7:14 does not refer to a *virgin*, or a *betulah* in Hebrew, but to an *'almah*, that is to say, "a young woman," a neutral term that does not necessarily connote virginity. For example, in the Song of Songs 6:8 the term "young women" (*'alamot*) appears in parallelism with "queens and concubines," who are surely not virgins. What is more, the *'almah* referred to in Isaiah 7, the young woman who in the near future will conceive and give birth to a son, is most unlikely to be a virgin. The context suggests that she is already married and is the wife of the reigning Jewish king, Ahaz, at the end of the eighth century BC.

By calling her *'almah*, the Hebrew Isaiah nowhere specifies that she is still a virgin or that the conception is foreseen to be miraculous in any way. The prophetic sign in the Hebrew Isaiah 7:14 consists not in the virginal state of the mother, but in the significance of the name she is to give to her son. The name "Emmanuel" intimates that the future prince, in conformity with the good omen expressed in his name, "God with us," will bring divine protection to the inhabitants of Jerusalem, who were threatened at that time by two enemy kings besieging the city (see Isa 7:16). Bearing all this in mind, one is bound to conclude that the Semitic tale underlying the present Greek version of Matthew in no way could comprise a prediction of the *virginal* conception of the Messiah.

How then did this notion enter the Infancy Gospel of Matthew? By sheer accident the Septuagint translator of Isaiah 7:14 rendered the Hebrew term *'almah* by *parthenos*, corresponding to "virgin" in Greek, though it may also mean "maiden" or unmarried woman who is not necessarily a "virgin." The "Greek" Matthew or the Semitic Matthew's Greek editor tumbled on this loose translation and adopted it. This godsend

enabled him to present to his Greek-speaking readers the conception of Jesus as unique and towering above all the other
miraculous conceptions of the Old Testament.

There is an incontrovertible proof that a substantial pro-
portion of the intended audience of the final text of Matthew
consisted of Greeks, who had no knowledge of Hebrew. In
Matthew 1:23 the Hebrew name "Emmanuel" in the Isaiah citation is furnished with a translation to explain that it means
"God with us." As one may guess, the original Hebrew Isaiah
includes no such interpretation, but more important, it also
lacks from its Greek rendering in the Septuagint. The Diaspora
Jews for whom the Septuagint was produced were expected to
know what Emmanuel signified. The Greek gloss in Matthew's
quotation, "which means, God with us," is manifestly the
evangelist's own creation for the benefit of his non-Jewish
Greek readers. So, applied to Mary, the Isaiah prophecy, as
worded in Greek, was intended to convey to the Greek-
speaking public of Matthew's infancy narrative that "Jesus–
Emmanuel" or "the Messiah–Son of God" would be conceived
of the Holy Spirit and miraculously produced by Mary *as* a
virgin.

The Greek Matthew consequently claims that the virginal
conception is demonstrated by the Isaiah citation. However,
the evangelist's argument is topsy-turvy. He wishes his reader
to understand that the event fulfilled the prophecy; in other
words, that the conception of Jesus by Mary happened because
according to Isaiah it was so predestined by God. The truth
is the opposite way around: the idea of the "conceiving
parthenos," supplied by the prophecy in Greek, motivated the
story. It was the Greek text of Isaiah 7:14 that provided

Matthew with a striking formula for expressing the miraculous character of Jesus' birth as the realization of a scriptural prediction.

To repeat it for a last time, the virginal conception is a historicized extrapolation of the words of the Septuagint, proffered to and understood by a Hellenistic Gentile-Christian audience of the Gospel of Matthew. The birth story of Jesus, told in Aramaic or Hebrew and quoting Isaiah in Hebrew, could never have given rise to such an interpretation. But in Greek, combined with the literal exegesis of the name "Emmanuel=God with us," it became the source out of which arose the concept of the divine Son of a virgin mother. It must be reiterated, even though this may be ad nauseam, that such a development was possible only in a Greek-speaking Hellenistic cultural environment. The ideological background of Graeco-Roman mythology and the legends relating to the divine origin of eminent figures in the recent past and in the present (see pp. 47–48) supplied a fertile ground for the growth of what was to become in theological Christian jargon *Christology*. In due course, this original idea evolved via Paul, John, and the philosophizing Greek Church Fathers into the deification of Jesus, Son of the God-bearing (*Theotokos*) Virgin.

That the idea of the virginal conception construed on the text of Matthew with its use of the Septuagint of Isaiah was of *Hellenistic* Gentile-Christian origin can also be argued negatively from the stance adopted on the subject by ancient Judaeo-Christianity. Important facets of the teaching of these Jewish-Christians, known as the Ebionites or the Poor, have been preserved in the writings of Church apologists who sought to refute them. Under the title "Ebionites," we have to understand Jewish-Christian communities which after their separation from the main Gentile-Christian Church, probably at the turn of the first century AD, survived for a further two or three hundred years. We learn from the late-second-century Church Father Irenaeus, bishop of Lyons, and Eusebius, the fourth-century Church historian from Caesarea, that the Ebionites rejected the doctrine of the virgin birth. Eusebius makes plain that for them Jesus was "the child of a normal union between a man and Mary" (*Ecclesiastical History* 3:27). Earlier, Irenaeus argued, using phrases borrowed from the New Testament, that the Ebionites were "unwilling to understand that the Holy Spirit had come to Mary and the power of the Most High had overshadowed her" (*Against Heresies* 5:1, 3). He further explained that in order to bolster their teaching and pull the rug out from under the feet of Christian orthodoxy, the Ebionites championed the Greek version of Theodotion and Aquila as more correct than the Septuagint, and substituted for the *parthenos* (virgin) of the Septuagint the term *neanis* (young woman) in their rendering of Isaiah 7:14 (ibid. 3:21, 1). In their view, the proof of the unreliability of the Septuagint sounded the death knell of Matthew's and the Christian Church's doctrine of the virginal conception.

Indeed, the *'almah* of the Hebrew Isaiah and the corresponding *neanis* of Aquila and Theodotion reveal the fragility of the idea of the virgin birth, as conceived by the Greek Matthew. Its adoption by the evangelist (or the final editor of Matthew) necessitated the revision of the straightforward wording of the genealogy (A begot B, etc.) with a view to excluding Joseph's paternity. It also has the unintended effect of spoiling the evidence built up to authenticate Jesus' legitimacy as Messiah directly descended from David through Joseph.

JESUS, THE *LEGAL* SON OF JOSEPH

Messianic status based on Davidic parentage and virginal conception—excluding Joseph from the real ancestry of Jesus— are forces obviously pulling in opposite directions. How have the Church and traditionally minded Christian scholars tried to overcome the difficulty? The most favored solution is the theory of legal fiction. Its holders advance the view that it was enough for Joseph to legally acknowledge Jesus as his son to confer on him entitlement to inherit the throne of David. They pinpoint the naming of Jesus by Joseph as the actual act of legal filiation. Indeed, according to Matthew 1:21, it was Joseph who was to call Mary's child Jesus.

It is dubious, however, to say the least, that name-giving amounts to the acknowledgment of paternity, and there is uncertainty in the New Testament tradition about the person who was the name-giver. The biblical proof text of Isaiah on which Matthew relies is of no use on this point. In fact, Matthew explicitly departs from the Septuagint, which, with its wording "*you* will call him Emmanuel," would have been pointing at Joseph as the name-giver. But Matthew's Greek quotation of Isaiah reads, "*they* will call him Emmanuel," an impersonal formula with no particular person in mind.

It is often alleged that the legal fiction theory is supported by rabbinic law, but the text of the Mishnah that is usually cited in support of it is of questionable relevance. The passage "If a man says, 'This is my son,' he is to be believed" (mBaba Bathra 8:6) is really concerned not with legal paternity, but with a particular aspect of the law governing leviratic marriage. As has been stated earlier (see p. 35), according to the biblical command, a brother-in-law is required to marry the widow of his deceased brother if he has died childless. The Mishnah introduces here a clause in favor of the woman. If the husband during his lifetime has called a boy his son—irrespective of this being true or untrue—his widow will immediately be free to marry any man she wishes, and will no longer be obliged to wait for her brother-in-law to make up his mind whether he is prepared to take her or not.

In short, the legal fiction thesis strikes very much as special pleading. Moreover, the tradition testifying to Joseph being the name-giver clashes with that handed down by Luke. There it is Mary, not Joseph, who is told, "You will . . . bear a son, and *you* shall call his name Jesus" (Lk 1:31).

PERPETUAL VIRGINITY OF MARY?

The doctrine cherished in traditional mainstream Catholic and Eastern Orthodox Christianity of the perpetual virginity of Mary, before, during, and after the birth of Jesus, is definitely not buttressed by the account of Matthew. (Luke's corresponding evidence will be discussed later in this chapter on pp. 67–68.) While the Greek Matthew advances the virginal conception of Jesus by Mary, it seems to contradict the belief that her virginity continued after the birth of her child. We must re-read

Matthew 1:25. There we are told that after Joseph had accepted the miraculous nature of Mary's pregnancy, that it had come about as the result of the action of the Holy Spirit, he refrained from "knowing" her "*until* she had borne a son." To unprejudiced readers, this verse signifies that, while in Matthew's account during the period of gestation Joseph had kept away from Mary, after the birth of Jesus they assumed life together normally, as man and wife. A similar marital situation is hinted at again by Matthew 1:18, where the evangelist refers to Joseph and Mary *coming together*. The Greek verb *sunerchesthai* (to come together) regularly refers to sexual union. It is used by Josephus (AD 37–c. 100) to describe intercourse between Amnon and his sister Tamar and between Absalom and the concubines of his father, David (Ant 7:168, 214). St. Paul employs the same terminology as Josephus in his advice to Corinthian Christian couples: "Do not refuse one another except perhaps by agreement for a season . . . but then *come together* again, lest Satan tempt you through lack of self-control" (1 Cor 7:5). From this it would follow that those who are styled by Matthew the brothers and the sisters of Jesus, namely, James, the brother of the Lord, Joses (or Joseph), Judas (or Jude), and Simon, and at least two girls (Mt 13:55–56; Mk 6:3), were the children produced by Joseph and Mary after the birth of Jesus.

LUKE'S STORY OF THE CONCEPTION OF JESUS

Luke's more extensive Infancy Gospel combines the story of the conception of John the Baptist (see chapter 10) with that of

Jesus. The miraculous-birth stories in the Hebrew Bible as well as in inter-Testamental and rabbinic literature suggest that some kind of special divine participation in the birth of the Messiah would have been expected in popular religious circles. Luke, by propounding the wondrous pregnancy of the mother of John the Baptist, anticipates, sandwiched between two slices of the Baptist's story, the announcement of the even more wondrous beginnings of Jesus.

THE ANNUNCIATION

Lк 1:26–38

In the sixth month [[of Elizabeth's pregnancy]] the angel Gabriel was sent from God to a city of Galilee named Nazareth, to a virgin betrothed to a man whose name was Joseph, of the house of David; and the virgin's name was Mary. And he came to her and said, "Hail, O favored one, the Lord is with you!" But she was greatly troubled at the saying, and considered in her mind what sort of greeting this might be. And the angel said to her, "Do not be afraid, Mary, for you have found favor with God. And behold, you will conceive in your womb and bear a son, and you shall call his name Jesus. He will be great, and will be called the Son of the Most High; and the Lord God will give him the throne of his father David, and he will reign over the house of Jacob for ever; and of his kingdom there will be no end." And Mary said to the angel, "How shall this be, since I have no husband?" And the angel said to her, "The Holy Spirit will come upon you, and the power of the Most High will overshadow you; therefore the child to be born will be called holy, the Son of God.

And behold, your kinswoman Elizabeth in her old age has also conceived a son; and this is the sixth month with her who was called barren. For with God nothing is impossible." And Mary said, "Behold, I am the handmaid of the Lord; let it be to me according to your word." And the angel departed from her.

In Luke the principal dramatis persona is Mary, not Joseph as in Matthew, and contrary to Matthew's focus on Bethlehem, Luke chooses Nazareth, the hometown of the engaged couple, as the original locale of the infancy story. He then moves them from Galilee to Bethlehem and Jerusalem and completes a full circle by bringing the whole family back to Nazareth.

The angel Gabriel, one of the four archangels of Jewish tradition—the other three being Michael, Raphael, and Sariel or Suriel—appears to Mary in her family home in some kind of daytime vision, and he informs her that she is to become a mother, and will give birth in due course to "the Son of the Most High" and the King Messiah, future heir of "the throne of his father David" (Lk 1:32–33; see also 2:11). To her puzzled question of how such a thing could happen when she does not yet share bed and board with her designated husband-to-be, Gabriel answers that the divine Spirit will play a part in her pregnancy and that she will bear a holy child. To illustrate that such a thing is feasible for God, he informs her about something else humanly impossible, namely, that her longtime sterile and elderly cousin Elizabeth is already six months pregnant.

Luke's account about the extraordinary circumstances of Mary is clear-cut in appearance. She cannot understand how she could bear a child as she is without sexual experience. However, after closer inspection the case is less clear-cut than it seems. In fact it is quite equivocal. For contrary to Matthew, Luke never expressly declares that between the annunciation and the birth of Jesus, Joseph abstained from "knowing" Mary. In consequence, in Luke's perspective, the conception of Jesus could be something not unlike the miraculous pregnancies reported in the Old Testament, which are all assumed to have been combined with normal sexual intercourse between spouses. Joseph could therefore be the father of Jesus, and the role of the Holy Spirit could consist in the special sanctification of Jesus, making him "holy" and "the Son of God." The courageous words of the well-known Roman Catholic scholar J. A. Fitzmyer SJ merit quotation: "When [Luke's] account is read in and for itself—without the overtones of the Matthean annunciation to Joseph—every detail of it could be understood of a child born to Mary in the usual human way."[8] Later, it is true, Fitzmyer felt obliged to abandon this statement in favor of a more traditional reading of Luke's text when he found himself representing in a debate the minority of one against the unanimous verdict of the eleven other Catholic theologians.[9] Some may think that it was a pity, but quite understandable during the papacy of John Paul II.

There are only two references in Luke supporting the idea of the virginal conception. The first figures in his Infancy Gospel where Mary continues to be called Joseph's "betrothed"—not his wife—at the time of the birth of Jesus. This has all the appearances of a gauche editorial emendation of the original tradition. The Old Latin and (Sinaitic) Syriac versions of Luke have no hesitation to call her Joseph's wife with all that the word implies. Matthew, as we have seen, is not afraid to designate Joseph as Mary's husband (Mt 1:19). The other passage is in the genealogy (Lk 3:23), discussed earlier (p. 33), where Joseph is downgraded to the rank of the "supposed" father of Jesus (Lk 3:23), which in the context also appears as another patent retouch made on second thoughts.

THE VIRGINAL CONCEPTION IN LUKE

Luke's description of Mary's miraculous conception, though independent from Matthew and from the Greek Isaiah 7:14, sounds definitely odd in a Palestinian context, but he reveals himself more than once unfamiliar with things Jewish (see p. 126 on Lk 2:22–24). When the angel announces her forthcoming pregnancy, Luke's inexperienced young Mary seems straightaway to understand that the words refer to the otherwise unheard-of idea of virginal conception. Hence her astonishment and disbelief: How could such a thing happen to someone who has never "known" a man (Lk 1:34), and how could she become pregnant and still remain a virgin? But, as many scholars have noted, this question strikes as quite inappropriate in the Jewish historical, social, and cultural setting of Mary. On the lips of a girl who is already bound by betrothal to Joseph, and whose wedding day must have been fairly imminent, the question put in her mouth by Luke does not make sense. Should she not have asked the angel to instruct Joseph to hurry up? All he needed to do was to expedite the wedding by taking her to his home at once? Something unsaid seems to lurk beneath the ill-fitting words of Luke.

The secret probably lies in the equivocality of the Jewish concept of virginity. Few if any readers of the New Testament, apart from those versed in rabbinic literature, know that in ancient Judaism there existed two ways to define a virgin. In one of these ways, to which we are all accustomed, a girl is a virgin for as long as she has not experienced sex. The Hebrew term in question is *betulah*, which in the first meaning is the equivalent of *virgo intacta*, a woman with the hymen intact. It is attested both in the Bible, for instance when Rebekah is described as a maiden whom no man has known (Gen 24:16), and in later rabbinic writings (see Tosefta Shebiit 3:15). This first kind of virginity terminates with intercourse. According to the second definition, the girl is a virgin until she reaches puberty. This second kind of virginity comes to an end by the onset of menstruation. The Mishnah, the earliest law code of the rabbis, defines a virgin in the second sense as a girl "who has never seen blood," and the text surprisingly adds, "even though she is married" (Niddah 1:4). The Palestinian Talmud formally distinguishes between the two classes of virginity, one "in respect of menstruation" and the other in respect of "the token of virginity" (Niddah 49a).

The matter had practical relevance and was not a mere exercise of clever hairsplitting, even though some rabbis were past masters in the field. In the Jewish society of the age of Jesus, with arranged "child" marriages, the question could arise whether the bloodstain found on the sheets of a minor (i.e., a young female who previously has not had a period) after her wedding night should be attributed to the breaking of the hymen or to her first menstruation. So if a girl past the legal majority of twelve years was married, although she was still prepubertal, it was theoretically possible for her to conceive after her first ovulation, but before her first period. Thus such a person could become—*mirabile dictu*—a virgin mother (virgin as far as the menstrual blood was concerned) and even possibly the virgin mother of more than one child, according to the saying attributed to Rabbi Eliezer ben Hyrcanus in the late first century AD (Tosefta Niddah 1:4).

The practice of child marriage definitely existed in the first century AD. The rule of the marrying branch of the Essene sect as described by the first-century AD Jewish historian Flavius Josephus verifies it. These ascetics, who unlike their celibate brethren accepted marriage, nevertheless expressly prohibited cohabitation between a sexually immature girl and her bridegroom. Marital practice could begin only after the bride had proved by three successive monthly periods that she was physically fit for conceiving. This proof was necessary because sexual intercourse was justified in the view of the marrying Essenes only for the sake of procreation. Consequently, sex was prohibited with a girl before she had reached puberty and even with a wife after she knew that she was pregnant, or no doubt after the menopause (Josephus, *Jewish War* 2:161).

In Luke's account, Mary's perplexity about the prospect of her imminent motherhood was alleviated by the angel assuring her that Heaven can cope with such minor matters, as is demonstrated by the case of Elizabeth (Lk 1:34–37). For God, it is no more difficult to enable a postmenopausal woman to bear a child than to allow a virgin, in the sense of a physically immature female, to conceive. In fact, a woman beyond the age of childbearing was called a virgin for the second time. Philo, addressing educated Hellenized Jews, likened the elderly Sarah to someone who had passed "from womanhood to virginity" (*The Posterity of Cain* 134). The logic of Gabriel's argument dealing with the situation of Mary and Elizabeth makes best sense if by "virgin" we understand a girl before reaching puberty.

On re-examination, the idea of virginal conception must be seen as a late accretion to the infancy narratives. Yet despite its special and unparalleled character, it has made no impact either on Matthew or on Luke, or on any other part of the New Testament. Its removal would not create a gap; it would not even be noticed.

We need to take into account the Gentile-Hellenistic context of early Christianity, with its heroes of divine origin, to reconstruct the background of the extraordinary beginnings of Jesus. Far the most important element in the puzzle is Matthew's recourse to the Greek version of Isaiah 7:14: A *parthenos* shall conceive. It served as catalyst in the development of the later notion of Mary as Mother of God.

By the beginning of the second century, when Gentile Christians became accustomed to considering Jesus not just as a metaphorical Son of God but as a divine person, his unique style of entering the human sphere would no longer create a problem. And when in the age of St. Augustine in the late fourth and early fifth centuries a convenient explanation was found for the universal transmission of Adam's original sin—the primeval taint was passed on from generation to generation through the act of procreation—Jesus' asexual conception by a virgin was the last piece completing a mysterious puzzle.

APPENDIX
The Question of the Illegitimacy of Jesus

The idea of the virginal conception and the mention of Joseph's worry about Mary's pregnancy soon produced a very much down-to-earth negative offshoot. Jews hostile to the Jesus movement saw in the birth story a deliberate cover-up invented by the early Christians to conceal the fact that Jesus was illegitimate. The scandalmongers of Palestine must have had a field day. They demanded a more convincing explanation than some fairy-tale story about an angel informing Joseph in a dream of how his fiancée had got in the family way.

Traces of the rumor are concealed under the surface of the New Testament itself. The allegation of illegitimacy probably underlies the altercation, reported in the Gospel of John, between Jesus and his Jewish critics. When his opponents protested that they were not born of fornication, they were tacitly insinuating that Jesus was (Jn 8:41). Also, some modern interpreters of the Gospels detect a slur in the designation of Jesus as "the son of Mary" by the people of Nazareth (Mk 6:3). One would normally expect them to speak of Jesus as "the son of Joseph."

The ancient copyists sensed a derogatory meaning in the phrase and sought to paper it over. They substituted the variant "Is not this Joseph the carpenter's son and the son of Mary" for the well-established reading "Is not this Jesus the carpenter, the son of Mary." But the proponents of the pejorative interpretation of the phrase "the son of Mary" may be mistaken. The occasional metronymic designation of rabbis found in Talmudic literature, i.e. the identification of a man through his mother, such as "Rabbi Yose son of the Damascene woman," does not seem to carry any depreciatory connotation.

Clear evidence of Jewish attempts to impugn the reputa-tion of Jesus by attributing to him illegitimate birth may be found in the Acts of Pilate, a Latin New Testament apoc-ryphon dating in its present form to the fourth century, but probably going back to the second. In it, the Jews decry Jesus as one born out of adultery (Acts of Pilate 2:3). The same charge is reported by the Church Father Origen, who states that according to the late-second-century pagan writer Celsus, hostile Jews depicted Mary as a poor country woman who was forced to earn her living by spinning after her carpenter hus-band had divorced her for being convicted of an affair with a soldier called Panthera (*Against Celsus* 1:28, 32).[10] Another Church Father, Tertullian, alludes to a hearsay propagated by Jews at the end of the second century about the mother of Jesus being a prostitute (*De spectaculis* 30:6).

The same calumnious charge is conveyed in a variety of forms in rabbinic tradition too. In the Talmud, Miriam, the mother of Jesus, was a hairdresser, the wife of a man called Stada, but she also had a lover by the name of Pandera. Hence Jesus was variously known as the son of Stada or the son of Pandera. For other rabbis Stada was the nickname of the mother and derived from an Aramaic phrase *sotat da*, roughly translatable as "that adulteress" (Tosefta Hullin 2:23; Babylonian Talmud Shabbat 104b). Similar polemical sarcasms are exhib-ited in the Toledot Yeshu, the medieval Jewish life of Jesus. The oddest revival of this idea comes from the most unexpected corner, the after-dinner conversations of Adolf Hitler, recorded by Martin Bormann. In them, the Führer asserted on a couple of occasions that Jesus' father was a Gallic legionary![11]

More recently, Jesus' conception out of wedlock has become a familiar topic of debate among adherents of the fashionable feminist school of theology,[12] though sometimes it is presented with the addition of a mitigating circumstance, namely, that Mary was the victim of rape. In contemporary literary theory the virginal conception is the "ecclesiastically correct" version of an awkward story about the mistreatment of women.

| 6 |

The Date and Place of the
Birth of Jesus

S O FAR, WE HAVE SCRUTINIZED WHAT SOME
would call the legendary elements of the
conception of Jesus and the aspects of the
story which are built on Bible interpretation.
Now we can turn to more concrete matters and
endeavor to situate his birth in space and time.

MATTHEW'S ACCOUNT

The infancy narrative of Matthew mentions
only summarily the Nativity itself. The evangelist supplies no details regarding the event
(see p. 53). The story of Joseph's discovery that
his fiancée was expecting a child is simply pref-
aced by the heading "Now the birth of Jesus
Christ took place this way" (Mt 1:18). A little

later he simply repeats: "Now when Jesus was born in Bethlehem of Judaea in the days of Herod the king" (Mt 2:1). Further elaboration follows when Matthew refers to the consultation of the Jewish chief priests by Herod in answer to the inquiry of the Magi (2:3–6). Herod's Bible experts unhesitatingly cite the words of the Old Testament prophet Micah 5:2, quoting from a Greek translation and not from the Hebrew original, but in a form that differs not only from the Hebrew text of the Bible but also from the old Greek version of the Scriptures (third–first century BC), attributed to seventy translators and known as the Septuagint (LXX = 70). In fact, among the twenty-four Greek words of the verse in Matthew's quotation and the twenty-one words of the Septuagint, only six are in common:

Matthew:

And you, O Bethlehem, **in the land of Judah,**

Are **by no means least** among **the rulers** of Judah;

For from you shall come

A ruler who will **govern** [literally **shepherd**] **my people**
   Israel.

Septuagint:

And you, O Bethlehem, **house of Ephrathah,**

You are **few in number** to count among **the thousands** of
   Judah;

From you shall come for me one

To be **the ruler** of Israel.

To produce a case as strong as possible, the evangelist did not hesitate to rewrite his proof text. He turned into a compliment the prophet's belittling remark, referring to Bethlehem as "*by no means least* among the rulers" instead of a tiny place among the clans or thousands of Judah, attested in the Hebrew Bible and in the Greek Septuagint. Furthermore, Matthew's quotation amalgamates the last line of Micah with 2 Samuel 5:2, with a view to incorporating the pastoral metaphor (shepherding my people), and thus hinting that the Messianic ruler would follow in the footsteps of the young David, the son of Jesse, who was the guardian of his father's flock in Bethlehem (1 Sam 17:15).

For Matthew—and the same remark applies to Luke too—the geographical setting is crucially important, as it has a major theological significance. Matthew is fully aware of a Jewish tradition according to which the Messiah is expected to come from Bethlehem. In addition to Micah 5:2 concerning the insignificant Bethlehem being the birthplace of the future ruler of Israel, we find, two verses later, an association between ruler and shepherd, and a little earlier (in Micah 4:8) reference is made to "the Tower of the Flock" or fortified sheepfold as the place where the dominion and the kingdom will be manifested.

The common Jewish interpretative tradition, represented by the Aramaic Targum Jonathan to the Prophets, identifies the "ruler" with "the Messiah" (at Micah 5:2; 5:1 in the Hebrew Bible) and the "Tower of the Flock" (at Micah 4:8) with the locality (Bethlehem) where the Messiah of Israel will inherit the kingdom (see also Targum Pseudo-Jonathan on Gen 35:21). The Palestinian Talmud combines the three elements—Bethlehem, Tower of the Flock, Messianic king—in declaring that the Messiah would arise from "the royal city of Bethlehem of Judah" (Berakhot 5a). The Church Father Origen (c. 185–c. 254) negatively confirms this tradition when he alleges that the Jews have attempted to undermine the Church's doctrine about Jesus being the promised Christ by attempting to suppress the evidence about Bethlehem as the birthplace of the Messiah. This statement seems of doubtful validity, for if these Jews really tried to efface the Messianic references to Bethlehem, they did a bad job, as a fair amount of testimony has survived until this day.

LUKE'S ACCOUNT

LK 2:1–7

In those days a decree went out from Caesar Augustus that all the world should be enrolled. This was the first enrollment, when Quirinius was governor of Syria. And all went to be enrolled, each to his own city. And Joseph also went up from Galilee, from the city of Nazareth, to Judaea, the city of David, which is called Bethlehem, because he was of the house and lineage of David, to be enrolled with Mary, his betrothed, who was with child. And while they were there, the time came for her to be delivered. And she gave birth to her firstborn son and wrapped him in swaddling cloths, and laid him in a manger, because there was no place for them in the inn.

Luke, in his turn, while asserting that Nazareth is the home ground of Mary and Joseph, takes the Bethlehem tradition for granted without adducing any biblical proof and makes Bethlehem the second focal point of the infancy narrative. It is there that Joseph and Mary are sent by the imperial census, and Jesus sees the light of day in a shed situated on the outskirts of the town. The word "stable" is nowhere explicitly mentioned. That the family was staying in an animal shelter is deduced from Luke's reference to a "manger" where the newborn babe was placed.

Bethlehem as the birthplace of the Messiah being a Jewish, and subsequently Christian, *theologoumenon*, or doctrinal prerequirement for the acknowledgment of someone as the Christ, it had to be verified in the case of Jesus. But as we have witnessed apropos of several other points, the theological demands of the infancy narratives—here the identity of the place of origin of the Messiah—remain without echo and support in the remainder of the New Testament.

Whereas Jesus' Davidic descent is a recurrent theme well established in the Gospels, especially in the Synoptics, his Judaean provenance seems to be more than once ignored or contested. People regarded him not as a Southerner, but as a Galilean born and bred. He was called Jesus the Nazarene, that is, stemming from Nazareth, or more fully the prophet Jesus from Nazareth in Galilee (Mt 21:11). Nazareth and the region of the Lake of Galilee were his *patris*, a phrase that can equally mean his place of birth, his hometown, and his home country (Mk 6:4; Mt 13:57; Lk 4:24; Jn 1:46). Apparently, some local Jews refused to accept him as the Messiah, precisely because they knew that he was from Galilee and not "from Bethlehem, the village where David was" (Jn 7:41–42). Moreover, they voiced the prejudice, no doubt of Judaean origin, that no great religious leader would ever hail from Galilee (Jn 7:52). So we must recognize that we are in an impasse: the birth in Bethlehem is asserted with theological certainty, but is queried on what seems to be factual knowledge.

WHEN WAS JESUS BORN?

As far as the time of Jesus' birth is concerned, only negative certainty is attainable; it can be taken for granted that it did not happen in AD 1. The traditional date resulted from a mis-calculation far back in the sixth century. A Roman monk, Dionysius the Small, a native of Southern Russia, tried to lo-cate the Nativity in a historical chronology based on the foun-dation of Rome. However, he erroneously placed the birth of Christ in the Roman year 753 AUC (*ab urbe condita*). It most probably happened, as will appear from the evidence, at least four years earlier. So paradoxically, Jesus was born "before Christ," "BC." This inconsistency is known to most people, but since it would be far too cumbersome to backdate every single event in the current era, the law of the least effort demands that things be left as they are.

Matthew in his birth narrative and Luke both inside and outside his Infancy Gospel supply sufficient information for an approximate dating of Jesus' arrival in this world. Matthew names Herod the Great as the ruler of Judaea at that time ("Now when Jesus was born . . . in the days of Herod the king" [Mt 2:1]), and Herod sat on the royal throne in Jerusalem from 37 to 4 BC. Matthew further alludes not only to Herod's death, which occurred in 4 BC, but also to his replacement by Archelaus, who "reigned over Judaea in place of his father

Herod" (Mt 2:19, 22) during the following ten years, from 4 BC to AD 6. The rough timescale is again confirmed by Luke's allusion to "the days of Herod, king of Judaea" at the opening of the infancy story of John the Baptist (Lk 1:5), and by his other references to Palestinian and international events associated with John and Jesus. He notes that Jesus was "about thirty years of age" at the beginning of his ministry, which followed his baptism by John (Lk 3:23). Then he laboriously identifies the start of John's career (Lk 3:1–2). The Baptist stepped into the public arena in the fifteenth year of the emperor Tiberius (AD 28/29), in the course of the governorship of Pontius Pilate (AD 26–36), under the rule of the Herodian princes Antipas (4 BC–AD 39) and Philip (4 BC–AD 33), and the high priesthood of Caiaphas (AD 18–36). (Luke's claim that Caiaphas shared the pontificate with Annas is an error. Annas was high priest from AD 6 to AD 15.) In the light of these combined data, we must conclude that if Jesus was in his thirties in AD 28/29, he must have been born shortly before the turn of the era. However, if Matthew's reference to the succession of Archelaus as ethnarch of Judaea is taken into account, Jesus' birth will have to be put back to some time before Passover in the spring of 4 BC when, according to Josephus, Herod the Great died.

But do we need these vague estimates when Luke clearly attaches the Nativity to what appears to be a major international historical event, the edict of Caesar Augustus ordering a universal census in the Roman empire, an order implemented in Palestine by Quirinius, governor of Syria? If we can fix the date of this *apographê*, or census, and the period of office of Quirinius as governor or legate of Syria, we will have deter-

mined the date of Jesus' birth . . . with the proviso, of course,
that Luke was correct in making it coincide with a census by
Quirinius in Judaea under Herod.

The event apparently alluded to by Luke is a universal census, or property registration for taxation purposes, imposed by
the emperor Augustus on the whole Roman world. The execution of the order must have been entrusted to regional governors, and this meant in the case of Palestine Quirinius, the
governor of Syria, Publius Sulpicius Quirinius to give his full
name. The evangelist does not explicitly mention Herod in this
connection, but the earlier reference to Herod's days (Lk 1:5)
implicitly defines the period of the census too. So we have a
Roman enrollment, implemented by a Roman official, in the
north and the south of the kingdom of Herod the Great, affect-
ing people both in Galilee (Nazareth) and in Judaea (Bethlehem).
It further follows that the census described by Luke is of a very
special kind. It requires people to make their declaration personally—not in or near the place where they reside and own
property—but in the town of their remote origin, that is, the
city of their tribal ancestor. For Joseph, purportedly a member
of the house of David, this meant, in the tradition represented
by Luke, a statutory visit from Nazareth to Bethlehem, the
city of David. And from the fact that Mary was in a very advanced stage of pregnancy at the moment of their departure on
an approximately seventy-mile-long exhausting journey—she
gave birth to Jesus when she arrived in Bethlehem—we must
deduce that her attendance in the company of her husband was
also thought by Luke to be obligatory. With the help of all
these details and in the light of our extensive knowledge of

Jewish history in the final stages of Herod's reign and of the ins and outs of Roman provincial administration, we ought to be able to pinpoint the precise date of the Nativity ... again providing that Luke turns out to be a reliable reporter.

Unfortunately, the Roman census will prove to be less helpful for the dating of the birth of Jesus than one might have expected. Let us begin, therefore, with the clarification of the terms. The Gospel speaks of a registration or enrollment of "all the world." Such a census, covering "the whole world," would deal with the countries of the whole Roman empire under Augustus with a view to furnishing information for levying taxes or enlisting men for military service.

However, there is no evidence that such an empire-wide census was ordered, let alone took place in the time of Augustus. Even if there had been an extensive census, it would not have been universal, as it would not have included Italy, whose Roman citizens by that time were exempted from the payment of taxes and from universal conscription. So the census could have only concerned the provinces of the empire, but no ancient source testifies that a tax registration was imposed on *all* the provinces at any one time. The nearest we come to such an idea is with an edict of Augustus instructing provincial governors to compile a list of Roman citizens (and Joseph and Mary did not belong to this class), but this was issued in AD 6, ten years after the death of Herod the Great, and consequently more than ten years after the presumed birth of Jesus.

So if there was no worldwide operation of any kind, was there at least a provincial census in the kingdom of Herod? The answer must once more be in the negative. Herod was a client king, a *rex socius*, and the Romans did not collect taxes directly from the subjects of such rulers. Moreover, we learn explicitly from Josephus that the Judaean kingdom was *immune* from Roman taxation for as long as Herod lived (Ant 17:27) and that Herod enjoyed independence in fiscal matters—so much so that he was even free to remit taxes when the Jews went through hard economic times. This Judaean immunity seems to have remained in force even after Herod's death during the ten years of the rule of his son Archelaus (4 BC–AD 6). It was only after his deposition that a census became necessary when a new taxation system was required in view of the recently established Roman province of Judaea.

Josephus describes the registration process set into motion in AD 6 by Quirinius, governor of Syria, in the former realm of Archelaus. It was a novelty so unprecedented and shocking for the Jews that it resulted in a major popular rebellion, fomented by Judas of Gamala, surnamed the Galilean. But the AD 6 decree would not have appeared such an innovation if there had already been a census a few years earlier in the final years of Herod. Besides, that particular census in AD 6 concerned only the domain previously governed by Archelaus, that is, Judaea, and would not have affected the Galilee ruled by Herod Antipas, where, according to Luke, Joseph and Mary had their residence. It is amusing to note that the Protoevangelium of James 17:1 tries to evade this difficulty by limiting the Roman census exclusively to the citizens of Bethlehem, assuming with Matthew that the parents of Jesus lived there!

Nor was it possible for Quirinius to conduct a census in the kingdom of Herod, not only because the realm of a client king was not subject to censuses but also because Quirinius was not governor of Syria while Herod was alive. Some scholars have sought to argue from a damaged Latin inscription, the so-called Titulus Tiburtinus discovered in Tivoli in the eighteenth century, that the Roman official mentioned there as having twice served as governor, but whose name is no longer extant, was Quirinius. Even if we accepted this purely hypothetical identification, the period of the first supposed Syrian office of Quirinius would fall in 3–2 BC, after the death of Herod. The slots in the governorship of Syria in the final years of Herod's reign are filled by Sentius Saturninus (10/9–7/6 BC) and Quinctilius Varus (7/6–4 BC). Since Herod died in the spring of 4 BC, there is no room left for Quirinius to act as legate in Syria, and definitely none before AD 6.

Finally, Luke's story about Joseph and Mary traveling from Nazareth to Bethlehem to be enrolled there "because he was of the house and lineage of David" appears to conflict with the sensible rules governing Roman censuses. Owners of property were to make their declaration to the censor in the chief city of the taxation district where they resided. This would have been Sepphoris for people living in Nazareth. They were not required to present themselves in the ancestral city of their clan, the distant Bethlehem for members of the house of David, where, according to Luke, Joseph surely had no house or land. If he had owned a place, he would not have been obliged—following Luke's logic—to look for shelter in a stable or a shed. Furthermore, the appearance of the head of the family before the censor sufficed: the presence of wives, especially wives on the point of parturition, was not demanded.

In sum, from whichever angle one looks at it, the census referred to by Luke conflicts with historical reality. According to the great Roman historian Sir Ronald Syme, the New Testament account is based on Luke's confusion of two notable events in Palestinian history, one dating to 4 BC (the death of Herod), and the other to AD 6 (the creation of the Roman province of Judaea). Each led to disturbances. The first followed the passing of Herod, and the second the census of Quirinius. More serious was the rebellion in 4 BC when Varus, the legate of Syria, needed the whole of his army to quell it. However, the crisis of AD 6 was better remembered because the imposition of Roman rule and taxation triggered off a long-lasting insurrection, launched by Judas the Galilean and continued on and off by his heirs up to the great uprising in AD 66.[13]

The mistaken placement of Quirinius' census in the twilight years of Herod is put to good use in Luke's narrative. It enables him to achieve his main purpose and transfer Joseph and Mary from Nazareth to Bethlehem so that Jesus might be born in the town from where the Messiah was expected to originate. The reliability of Luke from the point of view of historiography falls short of what one might have expected from someone who boasted that he had "carefully" (*akribôs*) investigated the records (Lk 1:3). Incidentally, this is not the only error of Luke in the domain of historiography. In Acts 5:37 he asserts that the revolutionary Theudas, who according to Josephus rose under the procurator Fadus (AD 44–46), *preceded* Judas the Galilean "in the days of the census." By putting him before AD 6, Luke predates Theudas by some forty years, a substantive error in what was in his days near-contemporary history.

Where do we stand, therefore, with our inquiry? The precise date of the birth of Jesus is still unknown. It occurred, it would seem, before the spring of 4 BC, and most likely in 5 or a little earlier.

In conclusion, regarding the date of birth of Jesus, we must be content with a *terminus ante quem*, pinpointed as the death of Herod. His birthplace is equally uncertain. Whilst Bethlehem cannot be absolutely excluded, it remains highly questionable. On the whole, a Jesus of Nazareth, the Jesus of the main Gospel tradition, is to be preferred to the Jesus of Bethlehem of the Infancy Gospels. Even in the most factual fields, chronology and geography, the birth narratives leave our historical curiosity rather unsatisfied.

| 7 |

Premonitory Signs of
the Nativity

❦

S O FAR, WE HAVE EXAMINED THOSE PARTS
of the Infancy Gospels which record
the annunciation of the conception and
birth of the Messiah–Son of God to Joseph in
Matthew and to Mary in Luke. However, the
good news is not meant to remain a secret entrusted to two persons; it was to be proclaimed
by various means to a wider audience too. The
means chosen by the evangelists are partly
miraculous, partly theological. Herald angels
are brought in to inform the shepherds in the
fields around Bethlehem, an unknown star is
seen by several astrologers in the East, and
Jewish chief priests and Bible interpreters
are summoned to disclose the meaning of a
prophetic prediction relative to the birthplace
of the Christ. Wondrous signs and portents,

frequently forecasting important births (and deaths), were believed to occur by both the learned and the simple folk in the non-Jewish world too. The accounts relating to Jesus are part of a much wider phenomenon and must be investigated in the general framework of the history of religions. Since Matthew's rich and complex story provides much food for thought and requires a comparative analysis, it is preferable to start with the simpler narrative of Luke.

A. Lk 2:8–20

And in that region [of Bethlehem] there were shepherds out in the field, keeping watch over their flock by night. And an angel of the Lord appeared to them, and the glory of the Lord shone around them, and they were filled with fear. And the angel said to them, "Be not afraid; for behold, I bring you good news of a great joy which will come to all the people; for to you is born this day in the city of David a Savior, who is Christ the Lord. And this will be a sign for you: you will find a babe wrapped in swaddling cloths and lying in a manger." And suddenly there was with the angel a multitude of the heavenly host praising God and saying, "Glory to God in the highest, and on earth peace among men with whom he is pleased!"

When the angels went away from them into heaven, the shepherds said to one another, "Let us go over to Bethlehem and see this thing that has happened, which the Lord has made known to us." And they went with haste, and found Mary and Joseph and the babe lying in the manger. And when they saw it they made known the saying which had been told them concerning this child; and all who heard it wondered at what the shepherds told them. But Mary kept all these things, pondering them in her heart.

And the shepherds returned, glorifying and praising God for all they had heard and seen, as it had been told them.

Luke recounts a simple tale for simple people. It starts with a heavenly sign, a bright light illuminating the night sky, and it is said to have been witnessed outside Bethlehem by a few guardians of the flock in the fields. They initially believed they saw one angel and afterward a multitude of them appeared. The first celestial messenger announced to the shepherds the birth of the Lord Messiah in Bethlehem. Then abruptly the whole angelic choir burst into singing glory to God and peace to the chosen among men. The second sign given to the shepherds is less spectacular: they will recognize the newborn king in question when they see a babe lying in a manger. One must presume that the evangelist located the place at the edge of the town or just outside it. This is how the shepherds of the story could quickly find people with whom to share the joyful news before they resumed their watch over their sheep. Luke's bucolic canvas fits well the image of the pastoral city, young David's Tower of the Flock, and evokes a scene of simple rejoicing among village folk at the news of the birth of a baby boy.

Three details in the story deserve further reflection. According to age-old local custom, shepherds kept their flocks out in the fields between March and November. This would place the Nativity not in the winter season of Christmas, but sometime between the spring and autumn. As has been noted (see p. 4), Clement of Alexandria (AD 150–215) testifies to traditions fixing Jesus' birthday on either April 20 or 21 or May 20 (*Stromateis* [Miscellanea] 1:21). This observation would be relevant only if Luke's description were historical, but obviously it is not. The second detail to reflect on concerns the end of the angelic praise, "On earth peace among men with whom he [God] is pleased" (Lk 2:14). The phrase *en anthrôpois eudokias* ("among men of goodwill") does not allude to people who are nice and kind. It is a Hebraism or Aramaism (see the Hebrew *beney retsônô* or the Aramaic *enôsh re'ûteh*, meaning sons or man of God's goodwill, in the Dead Sea Scrolls). The difference in the translation may not be of great importance, but it is significant that the expression clearly suggests a Semitic tradition underlying Luke's Greek. Peace on earth is proclaimed only to God's elect. The third point concerns Luke's statement about Mary pondering on "these things" in her heart. The most likely interpretation of the expression is that she was perplexed and was trying to puzzle out the significance of the arrival of so many unexpected visitors. The same meaning can be detected in a similar phrase appearing at the end of the episode of the twelve-year-old Jesus in the Temple (Lk 2:51). There again Mary is astounded by the words of her precociously wise son. Such an understanding of the verse is to be preferred to the traditionalist claim that Luke's report reflects the testimony of an eyewitness, namely, that it derives ultimately from the mother of Jesus.

Luke's low-key birth narrative depicts a simple and unspectacular rural event. Apart from the parents, themselves simple and poor Jews (see p. 126), it brings in only a few shepherds from the country and an anonymous gathering of local inhabitants, if we discount the serenading host of heaven hovering above the scene. This is rather a quiet welcome for the "Savior who is Christ the Lord" (Lk 2:11), but it may be a good prepa-

ration for the later emphasis in the Gospel on the blessedness
of the poor. Matthew, on the other hand, has arranged for the
king of the Jews a much more grandiose reception.

B. Mt 2:1–12

*Now when Jesus was born in Bethlehem of Judaea in the days of
Herod the king, behold wise men from the East came to
Jerusalem, saying, "Where is he who has been born king of the
Jews? For we have seen his star in the East, and have come to
worship him." When Herod the king heard this, he was troubled,
and all Jerusalem with him; and assembling all the chief priests
and scribes of the people, he inquired of them where the Christ
was to be born. They told him, "In Bethlehem of Judaea, for so it
is written by the prophet: 'And you, O Bethlehem, in the land of
Judah, are by no means least among the rulers of Judah; for from
you shall come a ruler who will govern my people Israel.' "*

*Then Herod summoned the wise men secretly and ascertained
from them what time the star appeared; and he sent them to
Bethlehem, saying, "Go and search diligently for the child, and
when you have found him bring me word, that I too may come
and worship him." When they had heard the king they went their
way; and lo, the star which they had seen in the East went before
them, till it came to rest over the place where the child was. When
they saw the star, they rejoiced exceedingly with great joy; and going into the house they saw the child with Mary his mother, and
they fell down and worshipped him. Then opening their treasures,
they offered him gifts, gold, frankincense, and myrrh. And being
warned in a dream not to return to Herod, they departed to their
own country by another way.*

In Matthew, too, the premonitory sign is celestial: a mysterious star appears in the East and leads the so-called wise men westward to Jerusalem. Matthew recruits a handful of distinguished visitors to pay homage to the Messianic infant. They come, bring their presents, and quickly depart. The ingredients of the picture are partly biblical, partly traditional Jewish, with a fair amount of non-Jewish spices and just a dash of dream à la Matthew completing the mixture.

The chief point of interest is the star. Ancient and medieval Christian tradition had no doubt about its reality. The simple and the great believed that the star truly appeared, was seen, was followed, and, having fulfilled its purpose, vanished from the sky. Even in more recent times, starting with the illustrious Johannes Kepler in the seventeenth century, astronomers sought to identify peculiar astral phenomena datable to the presumed period, which could have given rise to the story of the stargazers traveling to Bethlehem from the East under celestial guidance. An odd medley of theories has been proposed over the years to explain the star. It was a supernova; it was Halley's comet; or it was the unusual sight of the conjunction of Jupiter and Saturn. The first of these is pure speculation; the second was visible in 12 BC, a date too early for the birth of Jesus; the third could be observed in 7 BC, still a bit too soon. None of these explications would be very likely even if it could be assumed that the Infancy Gospels dealt with astronomically identifiable scientific facts, but the previous findings would make one feel doubtful in this respect. And what kind of a star, let alone conjunction of planets, could be followed from the Orient to Jerusalem, then for a few miles from Jerusalem to Bethlehem, where it would signal precisely the house among many houses where Jesus happened to be? Already, St. John Chrysostom (*Homily on Mt* 6:3) realized that no star could point toward a confined spot from a great height and thought that it must have come down and stayed above the house! Likewise the Protoevangelium of James 21:3 puts the star above the head of Jesus. In fact, all the available evidence shows that the miraculous celestial body, attested in a document most probably dating to the final decades of the first century AD, can be better explained with the help of literary rather than astronomical considerations.

The most likely sources of the star heralding the birth of the Messiah are traceable on the Jewish side to biblical traditions and in a broader Jewish and non-Jewish context to legend, folklore, and religious imagination.

In the Old Testament, the principal starting point for our topic is the famous prediction of the Mesopotamian non-Jewish prophet Balaam, contemporaneous with Moses, about a star rising from the Jewish race. The Book of Numbers 24:17 quotes Balaam as saying: "A star shall come out of Jacob and a scepter shall rise out of Israel." Already the ancient Greek translation of the passage speaks of a "man" as the realization of the metaphors of star and scepter. The theme is further developed in the Damascus Document from the Dead Sea Scrolls where the author, who was awaiting the arrival of two Messianic figures, recognized the "Star" as the priestly Messiah and the "Scepter" as the royal Messiah (Damascus Document 7:19–20). Likewise, in the Greek Testament of Levi the "Star" of the new Priest—the Priest Messiah—is said to arise in heaven similar to that of a king (Testament of Levi 18:3).

The popular interpretation of Numbers 24:17, preserved in the various Aramaic paraphrases or Targumim, expressly includes the word "king" and even "Messiah" as the title of the person symbolized by the "star." Historically, the passage was applied in the second century AD by the most prominent religious teacher of that period to the leader of the second Jewish rebellion against Rome, Simeon ben Kosiba, surnamed Bar Kokhba, or Son of the Star. Rabbi Akiba declared that he was the King Messiah (Palestinian Talmud Taanit 68d). In the New Testament itself the Book of Revelation makes Jesus proclaim himself "the bright morning star" (Rev 22:16; cf. 2 Pet 1:19).

But apart from the Balaam motif, Jewish and Christian traditions associate the birth of other important personalities with extraordinary light portents. We have already encountered the case of the shiny surroundings of Noah (see pp. 43–44 on Genesis Apocryphon 2; see also 1 En 106:2), and rabbinic literature reports the same about Moses, who at the moment of his birth flooded the house of his parents with light (Exodus Rabbah 1:22). The Nativity of Jesus is sketched in similar terms in the Protoevangelium of James: "[Joseph and the midwife] stood in the cave. And behold, a bright cloud was overshadowing the cave. And the midwife said [plagiarizing Mary and the Magnificat], 'My soul is magnified this day because my eyes have seen marvelous things; for salvation is born to Israel.' And immediately the cloud withdrew itself out of the cave, and a great light spread in the cave . . . And little by little that light withdrew itself until the young child appeared" (Protoevangelium 19:2).

THE MYSTERIOUS STAR

Although it may have existed in unwritten form throughout the centuries, the theme of stars heralding the birth of the great and the good is attested in Jewish literature only at the medieval stage. The Book of the Upright, or *Sefer ha-Yashar*, composed in its present version in the eleventh or twelfth century, reports in chapter 8 the appearance of a new star in the sky at the moment of the birth of Abraham. Examples harvested from classical literature close to the time of the composition of the Infancy Gospel of Matthew provide interesting comparative material. Pliny the Elder testifies to a general popular belief that whenever an important man is born, it is signaled by the apparition of a new bright star (*Natural History* 2:28). Suetonius (*Augustus* 94) cites in turn a certain Julius Marathus reporting that in 63 BC, some months before the birth of Octavian, the future Augustus, the public portent of a star forewarned the senate of Rome about the impending advent of a king. Republican Rome finding the idea intolerable, a decree was tabled in the Senate forbidding the rearing of male infants for the next twelve months, a reaction similar to that of Herod at hearing the news of a newborn king of the Jews (see p. 110). The same child, Octavian, was also acclaimed by the Roman astrologer Publius Nigidius Figulus as the future "ruler of the world." The stars continued to be bearers of good news, and another astrologer, Scribonius, prophesied an illustrious career for the infant Tiberius (Suetonius, *Tiberius* 14:2). Tacitus too mentions a brilliant comet seen in the sky which led the Romans to imagine that Nero's days were almost over

and a new incumbent was on the point of inheriting the imperial throne (*Annals* 14:22).

Stars could deliver a dual message; they could announce
death as well as birth. In this connection it is worth recalling
that the sudden rise of a comet on the first day of the festivities celebrating the deification of Julius Caesar was interpreted
by the Roman people as the heavenly confirmation of the
Senate's edict proclaiming his apotheosis: "A comet appeared
about an hour before sunset and shone for seven days running.
This was held to be Caesar's soul, elevated to Heaven; hence
the star, now placed above the forehead of his divine image"
(Suetonius, *Divus Iulius* 88). This is the "Julian star" (*Iulium
sidus*) that is hinted at in one of the poems of Horace (*Odes* I 12,
47) and centuries later it inspired Shakespeare's immortal lines
uttered by Calpurnia: "When beggars die, there are no comets
seen; / The heavens themselves blaze forth the death of
princes" (*Julius Caesar* II, ii).

In considering the star of the Magi, it is worth recalling
that about AD 69, shortly before the time of composition of the
Infancy Gospels, the established ancient belief in portents announcing the approach of a sovereign became the focus of attention both in Roman and in Jewish circles. The two great
Roman historians, Suetonius and Tacitus, allude to a rumor
which was going around in the Eastern empire announcing that
a ruler of the world would arise from Judaea. The Jews, engaged in war against Rome, took advantage of the prophecy
and interpreted it as applying to one of their compatriots, the
coming King Messiah. But Suetonius and Tacitus shrugged off,
with the customary Roman sense of superiority, the insur-
gents' claim. They maintained that the oracle was aimed at a

Roman, this being realized when the supreme commander of their forces fighting the Jews, Vespasian, was elevated to the imperial throne (Suetonius, *Vespasian* 4:5; Tacitus, *Histories* 5:13, 2). Josephus also refers to this ambiguous prophecy, which his Jewish compatriots erroneously applied to someone originating from their country. Josephus went further and attributed to himself the interpretation that the beneficiary of the oracle would be Vespasian, and he personally conveyed to him the news in the presence of Titus and two of his friends (*War* 6:399–401). The story is confirmed by Suetonius, who in his account mentions Josephus by name (*Vespasian* 5).

In such a context it is not unreasonable to surmise that the anecdote of the Magi and their star derived from ideas floating in the air among Jews and non-Jews during the gestation period of the Nativity narrative. By the way, we also encounter a star guiding travelers in Virgil's *Aeneid* (2:693), written about the end of the first century BC. The Magi were in good company.

THE MAGI

After this "deconstruction" of the star of Bethlehem, what are we to think about the "wise men" themselves, who observed and followed it from the East to the Holy Land? "Wise men" is the modern English rendering of the Greek *magoi* used in Matthew's narrative. *Magoi*, or Magi, were originally Zoroastrian priests among the Medes and Persians who had the reputation in the Graeco-Roman world of being endowed with the gift of interpreting dreams and foretelling the future.

Among other things, the forecast of the date of birth of Alexander the Great was attributed to them by Greeks and Romans (Herodotus, *Histories*, 1:120, 128; Cicero, *On Divination* 1:23, 47).

For Greek-speaking Jews the word *magoi* mostly had a pejorative connotation and referred to magicians. It appears in this meaning in the Septuagint and Josephus, synonymous with soothsayers and "Chaldeans," but it also designated dream interpreters (Dan 2:2; 4:7; *Antiquities* 10:195, 216). Philo in general concurs with the Hellenistic Jewish custom, applying the title for example to the sorcerers and magicians of Egypt (*Life of Moses* 1:92), but at least once he credits the caste of the Persian Magi with the scientific vision of the world (*Special Laws* 3:100).

New Testament Greek in general follows the same path as the Septuagint, Josephus, and Philo. In the Acts of the Apostles, Simon Magus was an ex-magician converted to Christianity (Acts 9:9), and the Cypriote Bar Jesus was a magician and Jewish false prophet (Acts 13:6). Rabbinic Hebrew also attributes a derogatory sense to the loanword *magosh*: according to the Babylonian Talmud, a Jew choosing a magus as his teacher deserves to be put to death (Shabbat 75a). So in general, the term *magos* has a pejorative meaning. There are, nevertheless, two exceptions to this rule in Jewish writings and in the New Testament: the first concerns Balaam, who prophesied about the star rising out of Jacob, and the second the Magi of Matthew.

As regards Balaam, he ended up in Jewish and in Christian traditions as the personification of evil. The rabbis very often designate him as Balaam the Wicked, and the various New

Testament references are far from complimentary (2 Peter 2:15–16; Jude 11; Rev 2:14). However, we find several flatter-ing comments too. Philo, for instance, depicts him very posi-tively as someone possessed by "the truly prophetic spirit" which cleansed him of "his art of wizardry" (*Life of Moses* 1:277). Josephus, in turn, notes that Moses did a high honor to Balaam when he recorded his prophecies and thus perpetuated his memory (*Antiquities* 4:158). Finally the rabbis, who on the whole are deeply critical of the Gentile prophet, nevertheless select him as the opposite number with whom to compare Moses, and remarkably Balaam emerges victorious out of every round of the contest (Sifre on Deuteronomy 34:10).

Now let us try to understand Matthew's thought. Though he never explicitly states it, he must have considered the Magi, who traveled from the East to Bethlehem, as the heirs of Balaam. How could they have recognized the star announcing the birth of the king of the Jews except from Balaam's prophecy about the Messiah which they had handed down among themselves?

Here the words of two Church Fathers deserve to be called to mind. For the understanding of Matthew's vision of the star of the Magi, Eusebius comments: "In the case of remarkable and famous men we know that strange stars have appeared, what some call comets or meteors or tails of fire, or similar phe-nomena that are seen in connection with great and unusual events. But what event could be greater or more important for the whole universe than the spiritual light coming to all men through the Savior's advent, bringing to human souls the gift of holiness and the true knowledge of God?" (*Demonstratio evangelica* 9:1). Origen in turn paints a splendid portrait of the

Magi: "It is said that from Balaam arose the caste and the institution of the Magi which had flourished in the East. They had in their possession in writing all that Balaam had prophesied, including 'A star shall come forth from Jacob and a man shall rise from Israel.' The Magi held these writings among themselves. Consequently when Jesus was born, they recognized the star and understood that the prophecy had come to fulfillment" (*Homily in the Book of Numbers* 13:7).

It is conceivable that another relatively recent event influenced Matthew and prompted him to introduce the Magi into his narrative. This was the visit to Rome in the late 50s or early 60s AD of the Armenian king Tiridates and his courtiers, whom Pliny the Elder designates as Magi (*Natural History* 30:6, 16–17). This Tiridates is said to have come to Rome to worship the emperor-god Nero in the same way as Matthew's Magi came to worship the newborn Messiah of the Jews. A further curious coincidence which may have caught Matthew's attention is a detail noted by the Roman chronicler Cassius Dio. After Tiridates had been confirmed by Nero as king, this group of "Magi," like the "wise men" of the New Testament, did not return by the same route as the one they followed coming to Rome (*Roman History* 63:1–7).

Thus putting together Balaam, the Magi from the Orient, and a star, which traditionally signals the birth of a great king, the evangelist had all the ingredients of his story. Moreover, as Matthew was keen on involving non-Jews in his tale, demonstrated by his introduction of foreign women into his genealogy of Jesus, the presence of Gentile visitors as the first persons to "worship" Jesus in Bethlehem makes the Nativity canvas conform perfectly to his theological intentions.

Matthew first brings the Magi to Herod's palace in Jerusalem. They are grand enough to have access to the royal court, and their inquiry about the birthplace of Jesus is answered by the highest doctrinal authority, the Jewish chief priests in charge of Temple worship, and the scribes who, according to Josephus, excelled in the "exact knowledge of the Law and their ability to interpret the meaning of the Holy Scriptures" (*Antiquities* 20:264; for the corresponding Egyptian commentators of sacred writings, see p. 113; for the interpretation of Micah 5:2, see pp. 77–78). The child is found in a house, a more dignified place than Luke's stable, and the presents are lavish.

At this stage Matthew's plot becomes rather naive. Herod, instead of calling on his informers and the police to find the potential rival, passes on the answer of the chief priests to the Magi and cunningly asks them to report to him all they have discovered after visiting the new king of the Jews. Thus the ground is prepared for the next act of the drama, Herod's decree ordering the massacre of the infants in Bethlehem.

Led again by their star, the Magi discover the house and Jesus in it. Curiously, according to the Protoevangelium of James 21:3, the wise men enter a cave, not a house as Matthew has it. They "worship him" there, i.e., pay homage to Jesus, and offer him "gold, frankincense, and myrrh." The gifts have biblical resonance associated with Solomon and the Temple of Jerusalem. Traditionally, incense comes from Arabia rather than Mesopotamia, the country of the Magi. In this connection I remember that in my far-distant student days two of my renowned teachers in Louvain, Robert de Langhe and Gonzague Ryckmans, argued that even the gift offered to

Jesus, which is designated as gold in Matthew's Greek, could allude to another aromatic substance in the light of a South Arabic inscription engraved on an altar of incense.[14] Be this as it may, later Christian tradition interpreted gold as gold, and together with frankincense and myrrh they were seen as symbols of the kingship, divinity, and suffering of Jesus.

Their purpose achieved, the Magi, like the biblical Balaam, returned to their country, but following a dream, as is the wont of Matthew, they chose a different route for the homeward journey, avoiding Jerusalem and Herod. Thus the evangelist found a convenient way to provide a psychological background for the edict issued by the deceived and frenzied king, which, according to Matthew's story, led to the massacre of all but one of the male infants of Bethlehem.

| 8 |

The Murder Plot

ATTHEW TAKES THE OPPORTUNITY of the clandestine departure of the Magi to inject again an element of high drama into the story, which before the visit of the "wise men" was confined to the family circle of Jesus. Joseph, after having gone through the agony of deciding what to do with the pregnant Mary, is now faced with a situation in which the life of the newly born baby is threatened by the power of the king. To resolve the matter, a dream providentially brings along an angel, who enjoins Joseph to run and escape with the child to Egypt. Duplicitous Herod, who intended to employ the foreign visitors for intelligence-gathering concerning the new king, realizes that he has been let down by them. True to his character, he explodes in fury and orders that at one fell swoop all the male infants in the Bethlehem district be wiped out by his sol-diery. This could be history, legend, or an amalgam of the two.

JOSEPH'S NEW DREAM

Mᴛ 2:13–15

Now when they [the Magi] had departed, behold, an angel of the Lord appeared to Joseph in a dream and said, "Rise, take the child and his mother, and flee to Egypt and remain there till I tell you; for Herod is about to search for the child, to destroy him." And he rose and took the child and his mother by night, and de-parted to Egypt, and remained there until the death of Herod. This was to fulfill what the Lord had spoken by the prophet, "Out of Egypt have I called my son."

In the plot as devised by Matthew, the solution comes before the problem. Joseph learns from an angel about the approach-ing danger, before Herod has realized that the Magi have slipped out of the country without reporting back to him. In consequence, by the time the edict of massacre is issued, Joseph and his family are already on their way to Egypt, where they are to stay for as long as Herod is alive. This exodus in re-verse brings about the circumstances which will allow the re-turn of Jesus to the Holy Land to be proclaimed as the fulfillment of Hosea's prophecy, "Out of Egypt have I called my Son" (Hos 11:1).

Matthew's utilization of the proof text is once more pecu-liar and serves his special purpose, but it differs in style from his handling of quotations on the two previous occasions. With Isaiah 7:14, the evangelist or his editor relied entirely on the Greek Septuagint against the Hebrew Bible, conveniently bas-ing his argument on the *parthenos*-virgin, and not on '*almah*-young woman, phraseology. Coming to Micah 5:2, Matthew felt free to turn his back on both the Hebrew and the Greek Scripture in order to create a new text which would be more suited to underpin his case. In Hosea 11:1 he was faced with figurative speech in a poetic passage: in the mind of the prophet, the phrase "my son" does not refer to an individual, but alludes to the whole people of Israel. The ancient transla-tors, the Septuagint and the Aramaic Targum of Jonathan, cor-rectly understood and interpreted the passage in this sense. They distanced themselves from the literal rendering and of-fered: "Out of Egypt I have called them [the children of Israel] *sons*": note the plural. However, this true meaning of the text would not have served Matthew's aim. He needed to formulate the prophecy so that it would unequivocally point to a single subject, Jesus. So he preferred to discard the official translation of the Septuagint and substitute for "sons" his own literal ren-dering of the Hebrew into Greek as "son." Admittedly, it is not wholly impossible that an appropriate Greek version of Hosea with a word-for-word translation of the Hebrew text had already existed and was reproduced by Matthew in his Gospel. We know of such a version in the second-century ren-dering of Hosea by Aquila, the renowned author of a verbatim Greek translation of the Bible. But his work was published some decades after the completion of the Infancy Gospel. However, in the light of Matthew's previous record of manip-ulating the scriptural text, it is more likely that the Greek wording employed in this passage was his own handiwork. In that case one may infer that just as the *parthenos*-virgin formula of the Greek Isaiah 7:14 prompted the story of the virginal conception, the Hosea text thus understood supplied the inspiration for the story of the flight of the infant Jesus to Egypt. Jesus had to be transferred to Egypt in order to allow God to summon his Son from there to his home country.

HEROD'S MURDEROUS DECREE

Mt 2:16–18
Then Herod, when he saw that he was tricked by the wise men, was in a furious rage, and he sent and killed all the male children in Bethlehem in all that region who were two years old or under, according to the time which he had ascertained from the wise men. Then was fulfilled what was spoken by the prophet Jeremiah: "A voice was heard in Ramah, wailing and loud lamentation, Rachel weeping for her children; she refused to be consoled, because they were no more."

On realizing that he had been deceived by the Magi, Herod, instead of establishing which child had been seen by the foreign visitors, a task not beyond the ken even of the dumbest village policeman, ordered the wholesale extermination of the baby boys of the neighborhood of Bethlehem from newborns to two-year-olds. This would imply that in Matthew's perspective the star was first seen by the Magi some months before their arrival in Judaea and that Jesus must have gone on living in his home in Bethlehem, perhaps for quite a while.

Once more Matthew wishes to present the event as fore-ordained by God, as the realization of a prophecy. On this occasion, unlike on the previous ones, he even identifies the prophet and names him Jeremiah, referring to Jeremiah 31:15. The link connecting the prophecy and the murder of the innocents lies in Jeremiah's mention of Ramah, a place not far from Bethlehem where Rachel's tomb was traditionally venerated. It was in Ramah that after the conquest of Jerusalem in the sixth century BC the Babylonians kept their Jewish captives imprisoned before deporting them to Mesopotamia. So poetically, Rachel in her grave was weeping over the boys murdered by Herod at the end of the first century BC, as she had done over their forefathers nearly six hundred years earlier. The Greek citation offered by Matthew is a peculiar abridgment of the Hebrew text of the Bible. It is not in agreement with any of the variations preserved in the Septuagint, but while the quotation is free, there is no sign here of any deliberately twisted application.

Is this story consistent with what we know about Herod's character and volatile temperament? Without any doubt it is. His record of atrocities was a matter of common knowledge in Matthew's time. The list of people whom Herod directly or indirectly put to death is endless: it includes the supporters of the Hasmonaean aristocracy and the members of the Jewish high court who had tried to judge him. A large number of his other victims were his close relations. He was responsible for the execution of his passionately loved wife Mariamme, her mother, Alexandra, and her young brother, who was briefly the high priest Aristobulus III. Herod also put to death Mariamme's grandfather, the high priest Hyrcanus II, and

Joseph, his uncle, who was also his brother-in-law, the husband of his sister Salome. To cap all this, three of his sons also became the casualties of his insane suspiciousness. Rumor had it that the carnage perpetrated in Herod's family prompted his friend Caesar Augustus to utter the famous saying "It's better to be Herod's pig than Herod's son" (Macrobius, *Saturnalia* 2:4,11; the emperor knew that trying to appear as a Jew, Herod abstained from pork). As an ultimate gesture of madness, he planned the murder of a crowd of Jewish dignitaries imprisoned in the hippodrome of Jericho to coincide with his own death and thus ensure widespread mourning and lamentation during his funeral ceremony in nearby Herodium. It was due only to his sister Salome's unwillingness to implement the outrageous order that the final bloodbath was avoided.

In the light of Herod's reputation for savagery toward his family, including his children, the legend of the massacre of the innocents is provided with a plausible background. Already, the work known as the Assumption of Moses, which probably originated at the turn of the era, depicts Herod as the king who "shall slay the old and the young, and shall not spare . . . And he shall execute judgements on them as the Egyptians executed upon them" (Assumption of Moses, 6).

Nevertheless, while the murder of the innocents is consonant with Herod's character and consequently could reflect history, there are strong reasons to suppose that Matthew's account primarily derives from a powerful theme embodied in the popular Jewish understanding of the Bible. The Exodus narrative, with Pharaoh's attempt to get rid of all the newborn Israelite boys, observed through the prism of Palestinian and

Hellenistic Jewish tradition, supplies the model for Herod's murder plot in Matthew's Gospel. Ancient Jewish literature, represented by Josephus, Pseudo-Philo, and the rabbis, recounts the story of how the parents of Moses and Pharaoh were informed in advance about Moses' destiny. From another parallel tale, preserved only in medieval sources, the reader learns about the miraculous sign announcing the birth of Abraham and his escape from the murderous hands of Nimrod. Matthew's narrative must be considered in its literary-historical context.

Let us start with the Bible. In the Book of Exodus the increase of the Israelite population was seen as a threat to the security of Egypt. Their numbers had to be reduced. So, motivated by demographic considerations, Pharaoh issued an atrocious edict ordering Jewish parents to throw their newborn sons into the Nile. Most of the children perished, but little Moses, floating in a reed basket prepared for him by his parents, escaped drowning. He was pulled out of the river and saved by the daughter of Pharaoh. This much is known from Scripture. What did Jewish tradition add to the biblical account?

THE INFANCY OF MOSES AND
JEWISH TRADITION

By the time of Matthew, in the late first century AD, the story had gone through various evolutionary stages.[15] We are informed by one of the evangelist's contemporaries, the first-century AD writer known as Pseudo-Philo, author of what we know now as the *Book of Biblical Antiquities*, or *Liber Antiquitatum Biblicarum*, that a significant novel feature entered the picture of the childhood story of Moses—the disclosure of his future role as savior of Israel and destroyer of Egypt. Within the family circle it was Miriam, the elder sister of Moses, who played the part of prophetess. Like Joseph in Matthew, she first had a dream, and in the light of it she conveyed to her parents the part her unborn brother would play in the future: "And the spirit of God came upon Maria by night, and she saw a dream, and told her parents in the morning, saying, 'I saw this night, and behold, a man in a linen garment [no doubt an angel] stood and said to me, "Go and tell your parents: behold, he who shall be born of you shall be cast into the water, for by him water shall be dried up, and by him will I do signs, and I will save my people, and he shall be the captain of it always."' And when Maria had told her dream, her parents did not believe her" (*Biblical Antiquities* 9:10). The same story is repeated in later rabbinic sources with the difference that here Miriam/Maria's prediction was acknowledged by her father after the birth of the child: "Miriam prophesied, 'My mother shall bear a son who shall save Israel.' And when at the birth of Moses the house was filled with light, her father arose and kissed her, saying, 'My daughter, your prophecy is fulfilled.'" (Exodus Rabba 1:22; Babylonian Talmud Sotah 13a; Megillah 14a).

But the Jewish legend was propagated in various forms, and the revelation was not always restricted to the close family circle of Moses. The Egyptian ruler himself, the antitype of Herod, learned what was to happen, and this knowledge carried with it important consequences as far as our perception of the Gospel narrative is concerned. Flavius Josephus supplies the most significant parallel tale in his *Jewish Antiquities*, which was published roughly contemporaneously with Matthew. For Josephus, awareness of Moses' part in Israelite-Egyptian relations inspired Pharaoh to sentence to death all the newborn Jewish boys. They had to perish in order to ensure the elimination of Moses. Such an understanding of the affair puts the massacre of the innocents in Bethlehem in an entirely different light, with an Egyptian interpreter of their holy scriptures standing in for the Jewish chief priests approached by Herod. "One of the sacred scribes [a *hierogrammateus*, a person with considerable skill in accurately predicting the future] announced to the king that there would be born to the Israelites at that time one who would abase the sovereignty of the Egyptians and exalt the Israelites, were he reared to manhood" (*Antiquities* 2:205).

Josephus further recounts (*Antiquities* 2:210–236) that Amram, the father of Moses, also had a dream in which he was apprised that his son would become the future redeemer of the Jews. Afraid of breaking the royal command, yet intent on doing all he could to save his son, he constructed a papyrus basket and entrusted the fate of the child to God. As in the Bible, little Moses was found by Pharaoh's daughter, who adopted the boy and persuaded her father to make him his heir. The obliging Pharaoh took the baby in his arms, but Moses grabbed the king's crown, threw it to the floor, and put his foot on it. The sacred scribe, who had foretold the birth of the liberator of the Jews, then realized who the baby was and advised the king to kill him. However, divine Providence in the person of Pharaoh's daughter quickly stepped in, and Moses survived—

as would Jesus too, despite Herod's edict in Matthew's version of the story.

The rabbis were also aware of a similar machination against the life of the baby Moses. Predictably, here too the story commences with a dream. Dreams seem to be essential in infancy tales, and in this one the dreamer is Pharaoh. "The whole land of Egypt"—the story goes—"lay in one scale of a balance and a *talya*, a lamb, the little one of a ewe, lay in the other scale, but the lamb turned out to be the weightier. Pharaoh immediately summoned all the magicians [the Magi] of Egypt, and repeated to them the dream. At once Yanis and Yimbres—Jannes and Jambres in the New Testament, or Jannes and his brother in the Dead Sea Scrolls (2 Tim 3:8; Damascus Document 5:18)—the chief magicians of Egypt, opened their mouths and said to Pharaoh, 'A boy is about to be born in the congregation of Israel by whose hand the whole land of Egypt will be ruined'" (Targum Pseudo-Jonathan on Exod 1:15). In short, the court wizards explained to the king that the lamb symbolized a Jewish infant who would become a lethal threat to Egypt. In Aramaic, the word *talya*, like "kid" in English, can mean both a young animal and a child.

JESUS AS NEW MOSES

When we weigh out the similarities between the Moses/Jesus and Pharaoh/Herod features in the Jewish texts and in Matthew, their parallelism strikes as compelling. It is especially strengthened by the role played by the official interpreters, the Egyptian sacred scribe on the one hand and the Jewish chief priests and scribes on the other. In the light of the accumulated evidence, we must conclude that Matthew's episode must have been modeled on tales with which both Palestinian and Diaspora Jews of his age were familiar. Its formation was further assisted by Herod's reputation as an insane and bloodthirsty ruler, capable of committing indescribable acts of savagery.

But apart from furnishing material for a gripping episode of the story of the infant Jesus, the Moses link also served an additional purpose. Moses in biblical and Jewish thought was both the deliverer of the Israelites from Egyptian bondage and the great Lawgiver on Mount Sinai. In the main Gospel of Matthew, Jesus performs the part of the new Moses with the Sermon on the Mount and its Beatitudes representing the new Torah (Mt 5:1–7:29). The so-called Golden Rule, "Whatever you wish that man would do to you, do so to them," to which the evangelist appends, "for this is the Law and the Prophets" (Mt 7:12), is Matthew's quintessential summary of both the Torah of Moses and the Gospel of Jesus.

Now in the same way as Jesus' identification as the Son of David, i.e., the royal Messiah, has inspired the Matthean genealogy in the Infancy Gospel, his portrayal with the traits and colors of the infant Moses prepares the picture of Matthew's final understanding of Jesus as the Revealer of the new law and the Redeemer of the world.

APPENDIX 1
Jesus in Egypt in Rabbinic Tradition

The sojourn of Jesus in Egypt has left no mark in his life story in the Gospels. It was, however, seized on by the rabbis in their anti-Christian polemics in the early centuries of the Christian era. In their view the Egyptian connection persisted long after the infancy period. Jesus' acquaintance with magical science, the negative representation of his miracle-working activity, is ascribed to his contact with Egyptian sorcerers.[16] Origen's Celsus makes these charges in the late second century: "Because [Jesus] was poor, he hired himself out as a workman in Egypt, and there tried his hand at certain magical powers on which the Egyptians pride themselves; he returned full of conceit because of these powers, and on account of them gave himself the title of God" (*Against Celsus* 1:28). Rabbi Eliezer also asserts that Ben Stada (a nickname of Jesus, see p. 74) smuggled to Judaea, concealed under his skin, formulas of incantation which he had learned in Egypt. The Jesus of the uncommitted Josephus, the "performer of paradoxical deeds" (Ant 18:63), becomes in hostile rabbinic circles—under the impact of Matthew's Infancy Gospel—Jesus, the Egyptian magician.

APPENDIX 2
Abraham's Birth Signaled by a Star

The following rabbinic folk tale, preserved only in the Book of the Righteous, or *Sefer ha-Yashar*, and other fairly late medieval sources, is similar to the story of the infant Moses. Because of its late date—eleventh or twelfth century—it is unsuitable as comparative material, but is not without interest as a theme of folk legend, exhibiting curious resemblances to the account of the Magi and the royal plan of killing a newborn child. The boy in question is Abraham, and the king seeking his life is the legendary Nimrod, "the first on earth to be a mighty man" (Gen 10:8–9). This is how the story runs: Terah, the father of Abraham, was the commander of the army of King Nimrod. Terah's wife had just given birth to a son, and the happy father, surrounded by his servants as well as by the royal sages and magicians, was celebrating the arrival of the baby amid festive eating, drinking, and merrymaking. The tale then continues: "And it came to pass that when they left the house of Terah, the sages and magicians lifted up their eyes toward the heavens that night, toward the stars. They saw a great star come from the east and run through the heavens. [This is the feature that brings the story especially close to the Matthew saga.] And the star swallowed forty stars from the four sides of the heavens. All the sages of the king, and all the magicians were afraid because of this vision, and the sages understood the thing, and knew that it concerned the child. They said to one another: This is nothing but the child, born this night to Terah, who shall grow and flourish and multiply, and shall inherit for himself and his sons the whole earth forever. He, and his descendants also, shall kill great kings, and they shall inherit their lands."

Next day they reported their vision to Nimrod and warned him about the danger, and, as is to be expected, the king demanded that Terah hand over the child to be killed. Terah, rather coldheartedly by our standards, gave the newborn son of one of his concubines to the king and took Abraham and his mother to a hiding place in a cave. He grew up there while the king and his magicians imagined that the dangerous child had been slain.

| 9 |

The Settlement of Jesus in Galilee

A. MT 2:19-23

ATTHEW'S BIRTH NARRATIVE ENDS with the departure of the Holy Family from Egypt and their unforeseen and last-minute improvised choice of the Galilean town of Nazareth for their new home. Matthew does not bother to give a hint concerning the duration of the Egyptian episode. But it clearly ended according to his reckoning in 4 BC, the year of Herod's death. A double reason is given by Matthew for selecting Nazareth as the place of settlement of Joseph and his family: the first can be described as historico-political and the second as prophetic.

But when Herod died, behold, an angel of the Lord appeared in a dream to Joseph in Egypt, saying, "Rise, take the child and his mother, and go to the land of Israel, for those who sought the child's life are dead." And he rose and took the child and his mother, and went to the land of Israel. But when he heard that Archelaus reigned over Judaea in place of his father Herod, he was afraid to go there, and being warned in a dream he withdrew to the district of Galilee. And he went and dwelt in a city called Nazareth, that what was spoken by the prophets might be fulfilled, "He shall be called a Nazarene."

Matthew reverts to the angel-and-dream motif, already used first to explain Mary's condition, and the second time to convey the warning of approaching danger from jealous Herod. Here we hear the all-clear sounding: Herod, the persecutor, is dead, Joseph and the family can go home. But immediately the siren sounds again: Beware Archelaus! He cannot be trusted either. The unexpressed reason for the mention of Archelaus is the assumption that without the danger constituted by his succession as the ruler of Judaea, Joseph would have retraced his steps to his former residence in Bethlehem.

In fact, by order of the emperor Augustus, Archelaus replaced his father as ethnarch, but not as king, of the territory of Judaea from 4 BC to AD 6, and Joseph clearly considered him as great a threat as Herod to the safety of Jesus. The historical truth is that, although Archelaus first tried to ingratiate himself with his Judaean subjects, he nevertheless soon let loose his army on a group of religious Jews, involved in an upheaval in the Temple during the week of Passover in 4 BC. Hence there was genuine reason to fear him. But Matthew offers no specific explanation for his unwillingness to allow for a return of the family to Bethlehem other than the general prejudice that a son is bound to resemble his father.

A final dream, this time without the mention of an angel, directs Joseph away from Judaea toward the north of Palestine, to the district of Galilee. But we know from Josephus that when Augustus reassigned Herod's kingdom to his heirs, the tetrarchy of Galilee was allocated to another son of Herod, Antipas (4 BC–AD 39), who was later described by Jesus as "that fox," and is said to have plotted against his life (Lk 13:31–32). So why was the presence of Antipas in the northern province not seen as an obstacle for Joseph to take up residence there? Why was only Archelaus regarded as a menace? The evangelist keeps quiet on this issue; he does not seem to have thought out all the implications of Herod's succession.

In fact, Matthew's Joseph had no real choice. He had to opt for Galilee because Jesus had to be associated with Nazareth. As has been noted (pp. 79–80), the entire Gospel tradition and Luke's infancy narrative tie Jesus as well as Joseph and Mary before him to this locality. Yet there was no special reason for preferring Nazareth. It was not famous; indeed, it was a totally insignificant place, never mentioned in the Jewish Bible or in Josephus (full of Palestinian place names) or in rabbinic literature. Even for St. Jerome, who knew Palestine well, having spent many years in Bethlehem in the fourth/fifth century, Nazareth was just a small village, a *villula* in Latin. The earliest non-Christian reference to it comes from a third/fourth century AD inscription found on the floor of a synagogue in Caesarea. There Nazareth is listed as the seat of one of the Jewish priestly divisions, resettled in Galilee after the destruction of the Temple in AD 70. The only conceivable reason for the evangelists (both Matthew and Luke) to bring Joseph and his family to this place of no consequence is that Jesus was generally known for his association with Nazareth, that he actually grew up there, or was possibly even born in that town.

Matthew had a better way of deciding the issue. He proceeded in his usual manner and presented Joseph's choice of Nazareth as a necessary move to fulfill yet another prophecy relative to Jesus, "He shall be called a *Nazôraios*, a Nazarene." Some of Matthew's previous biblical proofs have appeared difficult, but this is the slipperiest of them all. There is no single source named: the quotation is vaguely ascribed to several unidentified prophets. As for the prediction "that he shall be called a Nazarene," these words can nowhere be found in the Old Testament as we have it!

Some scholars argue that Nazarene derives from the Hebrew noun *netser*, meaning "branch," and cite Isaiah 11:1, "There shall come forth a shoot from the stump of Jesse, and a *branch* shall grow out of his roots." But the problem that needs to be faced is that NeTSeR and NaZôRaios do not derive from the same root. Other interpreters seek to base the prophecy on the story of Samson in Judges 13:5, "For the boy shall be a *nazir* [a holy and ascetic Nazirite who abstains from wine and from cutting his hair]." However, Samson is not a suitable type for Jesus, and abstemiousness was not one of Jesus' obvious peculiarities. His critics, with usual polemical exaggeration, called him a "glutton and a winebibber" (Mt 11:19; Lk 7:34).

The solution considered most likely assumes that the two forms of Greek words—*Nazôraios* and *Nazarênos*—are synonymous; both designate someone belonging to, or coming from, Nazareth. The evangelist needed to prove Jesus' connection with Nazareth, and he solved the problem by means of a vague and probably ad hoc manufactured prophecy, vaguely assigned to some anonymous prophets. In short, Matthew's odd interpretation of the historical reality gave birth to a prophetic proof whose sole aim was to account for the migration of Joseph, Mary, and Jesus from their Judaean home country to obscure Nazareth in distant Galilee. The linking of Jesus to these two localities is the primary task that faced the writers of the Infancy Gospels. Luke had to transfer Joseph and Mary from the north to the south to ensure that Jesus would be born in Bethlehem; Matthew faced the opposite dilemma—how to bring Jesus from the south to the north—from Judaea to Galilee.

B. LK 2:21-40

In contrast to the display of grandeur associated with the Magi and the element of danger generated by Herod and his men, Luke continues his low-key account of the Nativity of Jesus. After the story of the stable, the shepherds, and the ordinary villagers greeting Jesus, he recounts the brief period of peaceful existence of Joseph, Mary, and the babe in Judaea—no doubt in Bethlehem—before bringing them back to their home in Nazareth.

And at the end of eight days, when he was circumcised, he was called Jesus, the name given by the angel before he was conceived in the womb.

And when the time came for their purification according to the law of Moses, they brought him up to Jerusalem to present him to the Lord (as it is written in the law of the Lord, "Every male that opens the womb shall be called holy to the Lord") and to offer a sacrifice according to what is said in the law of the Lord, "a pair of turtledoves or two young pigeons." Now there was a man in Jerusalem, whose name was Simeon, and this man was righteous and devout, looking for the consolation of Israel, and the Holy Spirit was upon him. And it had been revealed to him by the Holy Spirit that he would not see death before he had seen the Lord's Christ. And he came in the Spirit into the temple, and when the parents brought in the child Jesus, to do for him according to the custom of the Law, he took him up in his arms and blessed God and said,

"Lord, now you are letting your servant depart in peace, according to your word;

for my eyes have seen your salvation

that you have prepared in the presence of all peoples,

a light for revelation to the Gentiles,

and for glory to your people Israel."

And his father and his mother marveled at what was said about him. And Simeon blessed them and said to Mary his mother,

"Behold, this child is appointed for the fall and rising of many in Israel, and for a sign that is opposed and a sword will pierce through your own soul also, so that thoughts from many hearts may be revealed."

And there was a prophetess, Anna, the daughter of Phanuel, of the tribe of Asher. She was advanced in years, having lived with her husband seven years from when she was a virgin, and then as a widow until she was eighty-four. She did not depart from the temple, worshipping with fasting and prayer night and day. And coming up at that very hour she began to give thanks to God and to speak of him to all who were waiting for the redemption of Jerusalem.

And when they had performed everything according to the Law of the Lord, they returned into Galilee, to their own town of Nazareth. And the child grew and became strong, filled with wisdom. And the favor of God was upon him.

Luke does not tell his readers whether Jesus and his family remained in the shed or moved into some more decent accommodation during the days which followed the birth of the child. The first special event briefly recorded is the circumcision of the week-old boy in conformity with the law laid down in Leviticus 12:3, "On the eighth day the flesh of his foreskin shall be circumcised." It was then that Jesus received his name, Yeshua in Hebrew, commonly used among Jews. Who the name-giver was, the father or the mother, is not stated. Tradition would allow either. In Matthew, as has been noted (p. 63), it befell to Joseph to play the role in accordance with the anonymous angel's instruction in his dream (Mt 1:21). In Luke, on the other hand, Gabriel entrusted Mary with the duty to name her son (Lk 1:31).

Naming a male child on the occasion of his circumcision has become traditional in Judaism, but the Bible contains no rules in this respect. Luke refers to the custom twice: first in relation to John, so called both by his mother and by his father, and then to Jesus (Lk 1:59–63; 2:21), and in doing so he supplies the earliest evidence associating the naming of a boy with the ritual of circumcision.

The second family feast day, combining the presentation of Jesus in the Temple and the purification of his mother after giving birth to a boy, severely tested the Gentile Luke's understanding of Jewish customs. The Mosaic law laid down that every firstborn male child should become God's property, but he could be redeemed from devoting his whole life to liturgical worship by means of a payment to the Temple of five shekels of silver (Num 18:15–16). Furthermore, a mother who had given birth to a boy had to undergo purification forty days after the event. The sacrifice which was to accompany the purification ceremony consisted of a one-year-old lamb and a young pigeon or a turtledove. However, if a lamb was beyond the family's means, two turtledoves or two young pigeons could be offered as a substitute. Luke mentions only the latter, the pair of birds, and thereby intentionally or unintentionally classifies Mary as not wealthy enough to afford a lamb.

As it happens, Luke gets almost everything slightly off-true. First of all, he refers not to Mary's but to "*their* purification." Whether he meant Mary and Joseph or Mary and Jesus, he was mistaken. Only the mother was liable to ritual cleansing. Next, he is unaware of the redemption fee of five shekels and confuses it with the sacrifice to be offered by the mother.

Be this as it may, the main message is that the parents of Jesus stayed in the south undisturbed by Herod—no murder plot, no flight to Egypt—and conscientiously fulfilled all the religious obligations imposed on pious Jews by biblical law.

Moreover, the visit to the Temple offers Luke an opportunity to indicate that God-fearing Jews, inspired by the same Holy Spirit who was instrumental in the conception of Jesus, recognized from the very beginning his future greatness. The role assigned to Simeon, apparently an old man, and Anna, a devout widow of eighty-four years, is to proclaim in advance that Jesus would become the future Messiah, the redeemer of Israel. Anna is explicitly introduced as a prophetess, and Simeon is portrayed as a man directed by the Holy Spirit. They are portrayed as divinely predisposed to recognize Jesus.

Luke further ensures that his own universalistic message—the Gospel to be preached beyond the boundaries of the Jewish world—finds an early expression. Not only is Jesus to bring salvation to God's people Israel, but he will also be the light of revelation to the Gentiles. Luke further inserts a hint about Jesus as a future object of contention, "a sign that is spoken against," in Israel. Instead of the imminent crisis signaled by Matthew, Luke concludes his infancy account by forecasting the future tragic—as well as glorious—destiny of Jesus.

After the completion of the Temple ceremonies, the pendulum returns to its starting point. Jesus was duly born in Bethlehem thanks to the obliging intervention of Caesar Augustus, and he can now set forth to Nazareth, where according to the prophets he belongs.

At this point the principal part of the Infancy Gospels abruptly terminates in Matthew, leaving a yawning gap of thirty years in his biography of Christ, and the story is not relaunched until we meet the grown-up Jesus just before he is baptized by John on the shore of the river Jordan. Luke's ending is smoother. As a parting comment, he foresees a happy future for the child blessed by God, and growing in strength and wisdom. He also appends an afterthought in the form of a single further anecdote connected with Jesus, which he dates twelve years later.

Thus the infancy stories reach completion, and the real Gospel, as devised by Mark, is ready to spring to life.

APPENDIX
Fulfillment Interpretation in Matthew

While Luke's Infancy Gospel does not use biblical proof texts to support its statements, Matthew regularly relies on them, and his first two chapters exhibit no less than five examples of explicit quotation, of which four are preceded by a formula indicating that the event in question was declared to be the realization of a prophetic prediction. The five citations are: Isaiah 7:14 in Matthew 1:23 (pp. 57–63), Micah 5:2 in Matthew 2:6 (pp. 77–78), Hosea 11:1 in Matthew 2:15 (pp. 106–8), Jeremiah 31:15 in Matthew 2:18 (p. 109), and an unidentifiable text of unnamed prophets in Matthew 2:23 (pp. 122–23).

The procedure is not Matthew's invention; it is common in the Dead Sea Scrolls and is also attested in rabbinic literature. The interpreters, especially those operating in the Qumran community, who created the Scrolls, expound the meaning of a prophetic passage by identifying the persons or occurrences in recent sectarian history and declaring them to be the implementation of ancient oracles. For example, the Nahum Commentary from Cave 4 claims that Nahum 2:11, "Whither the lion goes . . . ," when properly explained, refers to a

Seleucid Greek king's approach to Jerusalem: "[Interpreted, this concerns Deme]trius king of Greece who sought . . . to en- ter Jerusalem" (Nahum Commentary 1:1–2).

The Bible commentators of the Qumran community and the ancient rabbis attached their exegesis to the scriptural text as it stood before them. Sometimes they relied on readings which differ from the traditional wording, but as a rule they did not alter the scriptural sayings to suit their doctrinal purposes. Such a detached objectivity cannot be presupposed in the case of the "Greek" Matthew. Writing for a Greek-speaking Gentile audience, unfamiliar with the Jewish ways of treating the Bible, he not only felt free to twist the meaning of a passage to underpin his ideas—taking for instance the collective "son," which in Hosea relates to the people of Israel, as the designa- tion of an individual (Jesus)—but purposefully changed the wording of Micah so that instead of deprecating Bethlehem, it extolled its greatness. His free handling of the biblical evidence reaches its climax in the attribution of an otherwise unattested prediction about Jesus being a Nazarene, i.e., a man from Nazareth, to an obscure group of unnamed prophets: "that what was spoken by the prophets might be fulfilled, He shall be called a Nazarene."

In our discussion of the citation of Isaiah 7:14 as proof of the virginal conception of Jesus, we have posited that Matthew had been influenced by the Septuagint's imprecise rendering of *'almah* as *parthenos* (virgin), a rendering which was later re- placed by *neanis* (young woman) in the versions of Aquila, Symmachus, and Theodotion. However, in the absence of pre- Christian manuscripts of the Greek Isaiah 7:14, "Behold, a '*vir- gin*' shall conceive . . . ," a sneaking uncertainity will persist in one's mind whether the significant use made of *parthenos* by the "Greek" Matthew might not have played a part in the introduction, from the second century AD onward, of the word "virgin" into the *Christian* codices of the Septuagint translation of Isaiah.

| 10 |

Luke's Supplements to
the Infancy Gospel

⟶⟶❊⟵⟵

THE BASIC INFANCY GOSPEL, I.E., THE material contained in both Matthew and Luke, entails three topics: the miraculous conception of Jesus, his birth in Bethlehem, and the settlement of the family in Nazareth. This main narrative, thought to be traceable to a tradition preceding the Greek Gospels, was transmitted originally in a Semitic language, most probably in Aramaic, in Palestinian Jewish circles. The primitive tradition underwent further changes, first in Aramaic and later in Greek, as can be detected from a comparative study showing the discrepancies between Matthew and Luke. Other differences are attributable to the reworking performed by the two evangelists and/or their editors.

Luke supplies, however, two categories of additional material, totally unknown to Matthew. The first deals with the origin of John the Baptist and the second with a single incident
in the life of the young Jesus. Neither of them forms part of the
Christmas saga, but for the sake of completeness anyone inter-
ested in the Infancy Gospels must give them some consideration.

A. THE BIRTH OF JOHN THE BAPTIST

The relationship between the birth story of Jesus and that of
John is artificial and is undoubtedly Luke's creation. It is based
on the purported kinship between Mary and Elizabeth, a kinship that is never again mentioned in the Gospel of Luke or in
any other part of the New Testament. In addition to the family link, the common element is the intervention of the Holy
Spirit, who, after causing Mary's pregnancy, is said to have inspired Elizabeth to greet Mary, and to have mysteriously made
one unborn babe (John) recognize another unborn babe (Jesus).
Curiously, whereas Jesus is the leading actor of the infancy
drama, in the first chapter of Luke the space devoted to John
exceeds that given to Jesus. These peculiarities and the prehistory of the material relative to John ask for some clarification.

LK 1:5–25, 39–80
*In the days of Herod, king of Judea, there was a priest named
Zechariah, of the division of Abijah; and he had a wife of the
daughters of Aaron, and her name was Elizabeth. And they were
both righteous before God, walking in all the commandments and*

ordinances of the Lord blameless. But they had no child, because
Elizabeth was barren, and both were advanced in years.

Now while he was serving as priest before God when his division was on duty, according to the custom of the priesthood, it fell
to him by lot to enter the temple of the Lord and burn incense.
And the whole multitude of the people were praying outside at
the hour of incense. And there appeared to him an angel of the
Lord standing on the right side of the altar of incense. And
Zechariah was troubled when he saw him, and fear fell upon him.
But the angel said to him, "Do not be afraid, Zechariah, for your
prayer is heard, and your wife Elizabeth will bear you a son, and
you shall call his name John. And you will have joy and gladness,
and many will rejoice at his birth; for he will be great before the
Lord, and he shall drink no wine nor strong drink, and he will be
filled with the Holy Spirit, even from his mother's womb. And
he will turn many of the sons of Israel to the Lord their God, and
he will go before him in the spirit and power of Elijah, to turn the
hearts of the fathers to the children, and the disobedient to the
wisdom of the just, to make ready for the Lord a people prepared."

And Zechariah said to the angel, "How shall I know this? For
I am an old man, and my wife is advanced in years." And the angel answered him, "I am Gabriel, who stands in the presence of
God; and I was sent to speak to you, and to bring you this good
news. And behold, you will be silent and unable to speak until
the day that these things come to pass, because you did not believe
my words, which will be fulfilled in their time." And the people
were waiting for Zechariah, and they wondered at his delay in the
temple. And when he came out, he could not speak to them, and
they perceived that he had seen a vision in the temple; and he

made signs to them and remained dumb. And when his time of service was ended, he went to his home.

After these days his wife Elizabeth conceived, and for five months she hid herself, saying, "Thus the Lord has done to me in the days when he looked on me, to take away my reproach among men."

In those days Mary arose and went with haste into the hill country, to a city of Judah, and she entered the house of Zechariah and greeted Elizabeth. And when Elizabeth heard the greeting of Mary, the babe leaped in her womb; and Elizabeth was filled with the Holy Spirit and she exclaimed with a loud cry, "Blessed are you among women, and blessed is the fruit of your womb! And why is this granted me, that the mother of my Lord should come to me? For behold, when the voice of your greeting came to my ears, the babe in my womb leaped for joy. And blessed is she who believed that there would be a fulfillment of what was spoken to her from the Lord." And Mary said, "My soul magnifies the Lord, and my spirit rejoices in God my Savior, for he has regarded the low estate of his handmaiden. For behold, henceforth all generations will call me blessed; for he who is mighty has done great things for me, and holy is his name. And his mercy is on those who fear him from generation to generation. He has shown strength with his arm, he has scattered the proud in the imagination of their hearts, he has put down the mighty from their thrones, and exalted those of low degree; he has filled the hungry with good things, and the rich he has sent empty away. He has helped his servant Israel, in remembrance of his mercy, as he spoke to our fathers, to Abraham, and to his posterity forever." And Mary remained with her about three months, and returned to her home: *Now the time came for Elizabeth to be delivered, and she gave birth to a son. And her neighbors and kinsfolk heard that the Lord had shown great mercy to her, and they rejoiced with her. And on the eighth day they came to circumcise the child; and they would have named him Zechariah after his father, but his mother said, "Not so; he shall be called John." And they said to her, "None of your kindred is called by this name." And they made signs to his father, inquiring what he would have him called. And he asked for a writing tablet, and wrote, "His name is John." And they all marveled. And immediately his mouth was opened and his tongue loosed, and he spoke, blessing God. And fear came on all their neighbors. And all these things were talked about through all the hill country of Judea; and all who heard them laid them up in their hearts, saying, "What then will this child be?" For the hand of the Lord was with him. And his father Zechariah was filled with the Holy Spirit, and prophesied, saying, "Blessed be the Lord God of Israel, for he has visited and redeemed his people, and has raised up a horn of salvation for us in the house of his servant David, as he spoke by the mouth of his holy prophets from of old, that we should be saved from our enemies, and from the hand of all who hate us; to perform the mercy promised to our fathers, and to remember his covenant, the oath which he swore to our father Abraham, to grant us that we, being delivered from the hand of our enemies, might serve him without fear, in holiness and righteousness before him all the days of our life. And you, child, will be called the prophet of the Most High; for you will go before the Lord to prepare his ways, to give knowledge of salvation to his people in the forgiveness of their sins, through the tender mercy of our God, when the day shall dawn upon us from on high to give light to those who sit in dark-*

ness and in the shadow of death, to guide our feet into the way of peace." And the child grew and became strong in spirit, and he was in the wilderness till the day of his manifestation to Israel.

The preliminaries to the miraculous birth of the Baptist are unquestionably modeled on the story of Samuel in the Hebrew Bible (see p. 42). After suffering sterility for many years, Hannah, the mother-to-be of the future prophet, promised God that if he intervened and made her conceive a son, she would dedicate the child to the life of a holy ascetic or Nazirite (1 Samuel 1:11). God listened and fulfilled Hannah's prayer; Samuel was born and became a Temple servant at the Temple of Shiloh.

In Luke history repeats itself. The devout but childless elderly couple, the priest Zechariah and his wife, Elizabeth, play the part of the biblical Elkanah and Hannah. When Zechariah was on Temple duty, he saw a vision, and the angel Gabriel told him that his wife would give birth to a male child to be called John. He would be a Nazirite, always abstaining from alcohol, and filled with the Holy Spirit already in his mother's womb, he would be destined to become the new prophet Elijah.

Contrary to the young Mary, who readily trusted the angel, the more sophisticated Zechariah refused to believe what he was told and as a punishment he was struck with dumbness. In due course, John was conceived in the normal but divinely assisted fashion, and Elizabeth thanked God for removing her shame, as did the biblical women before her whose barrenness had been miraculously ended by God (see Gen 30:23).

After the interlude of the Annunciation, with the angel

Gabriel's mission to Mary in Nazareth (see p. 66), Luke introduces the episode of the visitation. No particulars are given
about how the pregnant young Mary traveled from Galilee to
Judaea (alone? in a group?). The traditional place of the meet-
ing of the two women is located at Ain Karim, west of
Jerusalem. In the neighborhood of Ain Karim a cave was discovered in 2004, and Shimon Gibson, the archaeologist in
charge of the investigations, believes that the site was used in
the early Byzantine period for the cult of John the Baptist.
Luke seems to interpret John's joyful kick in his mother's
womb as a sign of welcome for the few-weeks-old embryo,
Jesus, whom Elizabeth, no doubt believed to be inspired by the
Holy Spirit, subsequently calls "my Lord."

The song of praise—the Magnificat—which follows is ascribed in most ancient manuscripts of Luke to Mary, but other
textual witnesses attribute it to Elizabeth. With the hindsight
of almost a century, it is amusing to note that in 1912 that old
ecclesiastical busybody, the Pontifical Biblical Commission,
forbade Catholic scholars to adopt the interpretation which
places the Magnificat on the lips of Elizabeth. Yet the reference
to the low estate of the handmaid (Lk 1:48), corresponding to
the lifting of reproach imposed by men on sterile women (Lk
1:25), fits better the circumstances of Elizabeth than those of
Mary. Also, the Magnificat imitates in part the thanksgiving
psalm of Hannah in 1 Samuel 2:1–10, and Hannah is the model
of Elizabeth, not that of Mary.

But looking at it objectively, the hymn contains a good
many lines which have nothing to do with either Mary or
Elizabeth. "He has shown strength with his arm; he has scattered the proud in the thoughts of their hearts; he has put

down the mighty from their thrones and exalted those of low degree" (Lk 1:51–52) is more applicable to a war situation than to the state of either of our two women. Half a century ago, Paul Winter pointed out that the Magnificat as well as the Benedictus could be identified as hymns composed during the war of the Maccabees against the Greeks of Syria and not very skillfully retouched for its new purpose by Luke. What has become the Magnificat was originally composed to celebrate victory over the enemies of the Jews, and the Benedictus was a prayer before a battle. In fact, the most likely solution is that we are dealing here with pre-existent Jewish psalms similar to the hymns contained in the Dead Sea Scrolls. They consist of a cleverly combined anthology of poetic extracts from various parts of the Hebrew Bible. Recently, similarities have also been noted between the fragmentary Song of Miriam preserved in the Reworked Pentateuch from the Dead Sea Scrolls (4Q365) and some lines of the Magnificat.

In connection with the birth, circumcision, and name-giving of John, Luke mixes traditional elements with some strange comments. At the beginning of the narrative, Zechariah is said to have lost his speech. Later he is also depicted as deaf so that the family is obliged to use sign language to communicate with him. The relatives apparently intended to give the father's name to the son, as though this was normal. But I am not aware of the existence of such a custom in ancient Judaism. Neither did Palestinian Jews use writing tablets as Luke reports. Potsherds or bits of papyrus were their cheap writing material. Once Zechariah consented to call the boy John, he instantaneously regained the use of his tongue, a miracle that was seen as a good omen for the child's future.

The Benedictus, the thanksgiving hymn assigned to Zechariah, is as inappropriate in substance as the Magnificat. Its imagery is also bellicose and Messianic. It refers to the liberation of Israel, the lifting up of the Davidic horn of salvation against the enemies in remembrance of God's covenant with Abraham. Only verses 76 and 77—"And you, child, will be called the prophet of the Most High; for you will go before the Lord to prepare his ways, to give knowledge of salvation to his people in the forgiveness of their sins"—relate to John the Baptist and are obviously Luke's own composition. They are so formulated as to outline in advance John's future role in the Gospel (see Lk 3:3–5). The end of the section, Luke 1:80, also alludes to the prophetic destiny of the Baptist who will be "strong in spirit" and to his ascetic-eremitic training in the desert prior to his appearance on the public scene.

The life of John in the desert, feeding on locusts and wild honey, can be envisaged as solitary, like that of the mid-first-century AD Jewish holy man Bannus, whom the young Josephus chose as his guru. Bannus, he writes in his autobiography, "dwelt in the wilderness, wearing only such clothing as trees provided, feeding on such things as grew of themselves, and using frequent ablutions of cold water, by day and night, for purity's sake" (*Life* 11). However, since the discovery of the Dead Sea Scrolls it has often been suggested that John joined a communal type of ascetic group like the community of the Essenes. Nevertheless, if he ever did so, one must presume that by the time he launched his movement of repentance in the Jordan valley, he was no longer a member of the Essene sect, since it is known that the Essenes were forbidden to preach to outsiders.

It is a puzzle why Luke would couple his infancy narrative of Jesus with such a lengthy story of the Baptist. It has been advanced again and again that in fact he reused an extant birth narrative of the Baptist, originally handed down in the circles of John's disciples. There is no doubt that such circles existed; Josephus implies that John had many followers (*Antiquities* 18:116–17), and the New Testament explicitly testifies to it. John 3:25–26 alludes to jealous pupils of John who denounced Jesus to their master for baptizing on his own, amounting in their eyes to a unilateral declaration of independence. Moreover, the Acts of the Apostles records that the Alexandrian Apollos, Paul's associate, and some Ephesian disciples have joined the Church from John's baptismal circles (Acts 18:25; 19:3). They would have constituted the original audience for which the birth story of the Baptist was composed.

B. THE YOUNG JESUS IN THE TEMPLE

Lk 2:41–52

Now his parents went to Jerusalem every year at the feast of the Passover. And when he was twelve years old, they went up according to custom; and when the feast was ended, as they were returning, the boy Jesus stayed behind in Jerusalem. His parents did not know it, but supposing him to be in the company they went a day's journey, and they sought him among their kinsfolk and acquaintances; and when they did not find him, they returned to Jerusalem, seeking him. After three days they found him in the temple, sitting among the teachers, listening to them and asking them questions; and all who heard him were amazed at his understanding and his answers. And when they saw him they were astonished; and his mother said to him, "Son, why have you treated us so? Behold, your father and I have been looking for you anxiously." And he said to them, "How is it that you sought me? Did you not know that I must be in my Father's house?" And they did not understand the saying which he spoke to them. And he went down with them and came to Nazareth, and was obedient to them; and his mother kept all these things in her heart. And Jesus increased in wisdom and in stature, and in favor with God and man.

The anecdote appended by Luke to conclude his infancy narrative follows up his earlier statement about the infant Jesus in Nazareth: "The child grew and became strong, filled with wisdom" (Lk 2:40). The present incident gives an example of the intellectual prowess of the twelve-year-old Jesus. The occasion is the pilgrimage to Jerusalem undertaken by the extended family—parents and kinsfolk—on the feast of Passover. This was one of the three festivals at which every adult male Jew was duty-bound to participate in Temple worship in Jerusalem. The moment of reaching adulthood was determined by sexual maturity for both men and women. Girls, as has been explained (p. 55), came of age with the onset of menstruation, and young men with the appearance of pubic hair (Mishnah Niddah 6:11). From then on, they were obliged to observe all the precepts of the Mosaic Law, including the thrice-yearly visit to the Temple. Later it was thought that a boy attained legal maturity or the status of *bar mitzvah* (son of the commandment) on his thirteenth birthday. Girls ceased to be minors a year earlier. It would seem that, according to the tradition represented by Luke, male majority also started at the age of twelve.

Luke narrates that in the chaotic city of Jerusalem, filled with Jewish pilgrims as Mecca is packed with Muslims during the season of hajj, Jesus lost contact with Mary and Joseph, and his disappearance was not noticed until the end of the first day of the return journey to Galilee. The anxious parents looked for him for three days before finally finding the young man in what seems to be a school in the Temple. Jesus sat there among the teachers and took an active part in the discussion, showing in the process remarkable depth of sagacity and learn-ing.

Precocious wisdom is part of the pattern of a famous man in Jewish legend and tradition. About the young Moses, Philo of Alexandria writes: "Teachers . . . arrived from different parts, some unbidden from the neighboring countries and the provinces of Egypt, others summoned from Greece . . . But in a short time he advanced beyond their capacities . . . indeed, he himself devised and propounded problems which they could not easily solve" (*Life of Moses* 1:21). Josephus, in turn, boast-ingly remarks about himself, "While still a mere boy, about fourteen years old, I won universal applause for my love of let-ters; inasmuch that the chief priests and the leading men of the city used constantly to come to me for precise information about some particular in our ordinances" (*Life* 8).

In answer to the reproach of his worried and angry mother, "Your father and I have been looking for you anxiously," Luke puts on the lips of Jesus the following haughty words which foreshadow the attitude to his family of the Jesus depicted in the Synoptic Gospels, "How is it that you sought me? Did you not know that I must be in what is my Father's?" (Lk 2:49; see Mk 3:33–35; Mt 12:48–50; Lk 8:21). No surprise that Mary and Joseph were dumbfounded by the words of their provocative teenage son (see Lk 2:50).

Here ends Luke's Infancy Gospel with a reiterated assertion that the young Jesus continued to grow in wisdom and in favor with God and man. Accepting the pre-Lucan origin of the birth story of John, Luke's editorial retouches of the Baptist's infancy and the final anecdote concerning the young Jesus can best be understood as further preliminaries to the already fully formulated account of the Gospel drama in which Jesus of Nazareth is the star and John the Baptist plays only a supporting role.

Epilogue

THE INFANCY GOSPELS IN RETROSPECT

Having followed in the previous chapters step by step the unfolding of the Infancy Gospels, and completed a painstaking literary and historical analysis of their numerous particulars, we have now a clear idea of the individual details of the birth story of Jesus, but do we know what they all add up to? For what purpose were these narratives devised? Are they part of the original composition or were they affixed later to the Gospels of Matthew and Luke? Above all, where does history end and legend begin? To sum up our investigation and assess the significance of the two birth narratives, we have to find answers to the following five questions:

1. What are the Infancy Gospels?
2. How do they relate to the main Gospels of Matthew and Luke?
3. When and why were they attached to them?

4. What can they reveal about their prehistory?
5. What is their historical value and theological significance?

1. WHAT ARE THE INFANCY GOSPELS?

The Infancy Gospels are two parallel narratives, intended to recount the earliest period of the life of Jesus, starting with his conception and terminating with his arrival in Nazareth in the company of Joseph and Mary. The two accounts do not derive from one another. They have a few basic elements in common (extraordinary pregnancy, Bethlehem as birthplace, Nazareth as permanent residence), but they display a much larger amount of divergent features.

Let us consider the differences between the two accounts. The original residence of Mary and Joseph is not stated in Matthew, but as the only travel involved prior to the journey to Galilee is the flight to Egypt, it must be Bethlehem. By contrast, in Luke Joseph and Mary had been living in Nazareth and made their way to Bethlehem only to comply with the obligation imposed on them by Augustus' order of a universal census. The newborn Jesus was welcomed in a stable by angels, local shepherds, and townspeople according to Luke, while in Matthew he was worshipped in a house by the Magi. The interval between the birth of Jesus and his arrival in Nazareth entails in Matthew the escape to Egypt to avoid Herod's soldiers and a change of plan during the return trip demanding the migration from Judaea to Galilee, whereas in Luke Jesus, Mary, and Joseph retrace their steps to the original

hometown of the parents in Nazareth after forty days spent
peacefully in Bethlehem and Jerusalem.

2. HOW DO THE BIRTH NARRATIVES
RELATE TO THE MAIN GOSPELS?

When considered against the principal account of the life of
Jesus contained in Matthew chapters 3–28 and Luke chapters
3–24, the two infancy narratives stand apart and the bond linking them to the rest of the Gospel narratives appears extremely
flimsy. If the first two chapters of Matthew and Luke had been
lost, their disappearance would not be felt by the readers of the
main story. The latter never refers back to events already recounted in the opening section; it simply has no awareness
whatsoever of the infancy tales.

Let us change our point of view and look from the infancy
accounts toward the main Gospels. None of the major items
listed in the birth narratives is developed or even hinted at in
the subsequent life of Jesus. In vain would you rummage
through every line of Matthew or Luke to find a direct or even
a veiled allusion to the miraculous conception of Jesus or his
birth in Bethlehem, to the star and the wise men, to the immediate recognition of Jesus as the future Messiah by angels,
shepherds, or townsfolk, or by Simeon and Anna. Not even
the apparently weighty matters of Joseph's intention to divorce Mary or the flight of the family to Egypt is ever remembered. If the main Gospel tradition had been aware of the
wondrous features of the birth canvas, one would have expected to find here and there an innuendo to them, for instance

when the people of Nazareth were discussing the origin of Jesus or on the occasion of debates about his messianic status.

On the other hand, the Infancy Gospels are acquainted with the main accounts of Matthew and Luke and display a number of significant traits which are characteristic of the picture of Jesus in them. In particular, in both Matthew and Luke Jesus is portrayed as the Son of Abraham, the Son of David, and the Son of God. In Matthew he appears also as the new Moses.

The Son of Abraham title underlines the Jewishness of Jesus, through his descent from the father of the Hebrew nation. It appears in both infancy narratives, but in Matthew the motif is given a salient position and figures already in the title of the Gospel: "The book of the genealogy of Jesus . . . the son of Abraham," and Abraham is, in addition, the absolute starting point of the Matthean genealogy. Jesus is also portrayed as the future savior of his people by the angel addressing Joseph in his dream. This focus on Judaism is fully in line with the insistence in Matthew's main Gospel, or at least in the initial orientation of the main Gospel, on the exclusively Jewish direction of the ministry of Jesus and of his disciples, sent only to "the lost sheep of the house of Israel" and not to the Gentiles or the Samaritans (Mt 10:5–6). But Matthew's infancy story also incorporates two elements which afford an opening toward the nations of the world. Non-Jewish women figure in the genealogical table of Jesus (see pp. 22–23) and the Gentile Magi are the first to recognize and greet him (p. 99). This broadening of Matthew's outlook appears to reflect the evangelist's increasing disappointment with the Jewish response to the apostolic preaching and his later optimism regarding the mission to non-Jews which sees the Gospel more and more aimed toward the pagan world and depicts the messianic banquet as attended almost exclusively by Gentiles (Mt 8:11–12).

In Luke's list, Abraham is not brought into such a pronounced relief. He is just one of the many ancestors of Jesus. On the other hand, this non-Jewish evangelist includes in the birth story of Jesus the Mosaic customs of circumcision, the redemption of the firstborn, and the purification of the mother forty days after giving birth to a male child; moreover he makes his devout elderly Simeon depict Jesus as "the light . . . for the glory of Israel" and inserts into his narrative the episode of Jesus' Passover pilgrimage to the Temple of Jerusalem, a Jewish custom par excellence. Nevertheless, this emphasis on Jewishness is balanced by a universalistic trend. Luke traces Jesus' family line not just to Abraham but back to Adam, the father of all mankind, and in the Nunc Dimittis hymn Simeon characterizes Jesus as "a light for revelation to the Gentiles." The same kind of universalism is present throughout in the Gospel of Luke, for instance in the mandate of Jesus to preach repentance and forgiveness to all the nations (Lk 24:47), and in the repeated omission of references to Jewish exclusiveness like the harsh words of Jesus addressed to the Syro-Phoenician woman (Mk 7:27; Mt 15:26) or his description of Gentiles as dogs or swine (Mt 7:6).

The second characteristic title of Jesus in the Infancy Gospels is that of Son of David, which indicates the messianic dignity attributed to him. In Matthew, Messiahship figures in the title of the Gospel: "The book of the genealogy of Jesus Christ, the son of David" and King David stands at the head of the second group of fourteen generations, Abraham having opened the first. The Davidic descent is further stressed by Matthew when he adduces the biblical proof text of Micah, associating the birthplace of Jesus with the city of David, Bethlehem. Luke, even though he places no special emphasis on David in the genealogy of Jesus, similarly insists on his messianic future when the angel Gabriel promises to Mary that her child would inherit the royal throne and when the shepherds are informed about the birth of "Christ the Lord" in "the city of David." The messianic theme that dominates the main Gospels of Matthew and Luke, as well as Mark and John, is thus firmly anticipated in the birth narratives.

The third title in the Infancy Gospels, "Son of God," is a metaphor frequently encountered in the Hebrew Bible (see pp. 45–46), but Matthew and Luke and the rest of the New Testament have endowed the phrase with a meaning stronger than it usually carries in Jewish writings. Matthew applies to Jesus the name "God with us," the Emmanuel of Isaiah 7:14, and claims that in him were fulfilled the divine words uttered by Hosea, "Out of Egypt have I called my Son." For Luke, too, the child borne by Mary is "the Son of the Most High" and "the Son of God." This general elevation of Jesus, Son of David or Messiah, seemingly to a superhuman dignity, apparently starts from the extraordinary beginnings attributed to him in the Infancy Gospels. Early Christian legends progressively developing from the mid-second to the sixth centuries, for instance those recorded in the Greek Infancy Gospel of Thomas, portray the small child Jesus as healing the sick, raising the dead, and even causing clay sparrows to take to the air, but occasionally also abusing his divine miracle-working power by striking dead a child who semi-accidentally had hit him with a stone.

The wonderful birth stories of the Hebrew Bible, as well as those of the literature representing Jewish religious thought in the age of Jesus, suggest that popular circles would have found it normal that the birth of the Messiah should display signs of special divine intervention. In this vein Luke, by propounding the wondrous pregnancy of the mother of John the Baptist, paves the way for the announcement of the even more marvelous beginnings of Jesus. Both infancy narratives identify the Holy Spirit as the arcane medium through which the virgin Mary conceives her son. This seems to have amounted in Matthew's final version of the story to a miraculous impregnation without the sperm of a human male, leading to the birth of the Son of God in fulfillment of the prophecy, "A virgin [*qua* virgin] shall conceive and bear a son"—Emmanuel, or "God with us." By contrast, the version underlying Luke's account may have to do with the extraordinary pregnancy, in a normal marital framework, of a girl not yet physically fit for motherhood. Essential elements of this mode of thinking are implicit in Luke's words, establishing an opposite parallelism between the way young Mary and the senescent Elizabeth became pregnant (Lk 1:34–37).

A fourth unformulated theological feature, prefiguring the notion of Jesus as another Moses, is contained in Matthew's story. It derives from the biblical and postbiblical portrayal of the origins of Moses on which Matthew's account of Herod's murder plot against Jesus and the latter's escape to Egypt are shaped. The Jewish Moses motif, typifying the future prophet, legislator, and liberator of Israel, prefigures the picture embedded in the main Gospel of Matthew representing Jesus as the lawgiver and savior of his people. In other words, the "new Moses" feature of the Infancy Gospel supplies an ad-vance insight into the future destiny of Jesus as perceived by the evangelist, especially in depicting Jesus' proclamation of the Sermon on the Mount as a reenactment of the revelation of the Law by Moses at Mount Sinai (Mt 5:1–7:29).

In short, the three principal aspects common to both in-fancy narratives and the additional new Moses image in Matthew serve as connecting links which prepare and provide with a special perspective the full understanding of the Gospel message conveyed by the two evangelists. Luke's further sup-plements relating to the role of John the Baptist and the growth of Jesus in wisdom and grace reinforce the same con-clusion.

3. WHEN AND WHY WERE THE BIRTH NARRATIVES ATTACHED TO THE GOSPELS?

The two principal properties of the infancy narratives, their anticipatory character in relation to the evolved message of Matthew and Luke and the fact that their peculiar feats are to-tally absent from the main body of the story of Jesus, demon-strate that they are later additions to the main Gospel account. Some of the elements, especially Matthew's various scriptural quotations and the idea of the virginal conception in direct con-flict with the Judaeo-Christian tradition, make sense only if we envisage a second stage in the transmission of the Gospel mes-sage with the help of a Greek text and for the benefit of a

Gentile Hellenic audience. The stress on universalism in Luke and even more so in Matthew is a further argument in favor of a relatively advanced date for the emergence of the infancy addenda. Finally, the ultimate proof that the birth story is not a natural introductory section of a biography is the absence of continuity between it and the rest of the Gospel. If we disregard the odd episode of the twelve-year-old Jesus' Passover pilgrimage to Jerusalem, none of the evangelists accounts for the three decades or so that separate the infancy of Jesus from his adulthood.

Observing them with the benefit of hindsight, the ultimate purpose of the Infancy Gospels seems to be the creation of a prologue, enveloping the newborn Jesus with an aura of marvel and enigma (mysterious conception, wonderful star, angelic messengers, and revelatory dreams). This prologue forms the appropriate counterpart of the equally wondrous epilogue of the Gospels—also replete with angels, visions, and apparitions—the resurrection of Jesus.

4. WHAT CAN THE INFANCY GOSPELS REVEAL ABOUT THEIR PREHISTORY?

No doubt any attempt to venture into the obscure antecedents of the infancy narratives will carry with it even more speculation than we have been accustomed to so far. Nevertheless, let us proceed on the basis of as much evidence as can be mustered. Clearly, the two most fundamental points the birth narratives endeavor to make concern Jesus' messianic dignity (he is the Son of David) and his special relationship to the Deity (he is the

Son of God). We must also take it for granted that the original elements of both these features sprang from a Galilean milieu and were expressed in the language and terminology of Palestinian Jews who spoke Aramaic or Hebrew or both.

It is clear that in Matthew as well as in Luke the first and foremost attribute of the infant Jesus is that he is the future savior of Israel, the royal Messiah, Son of David. Two genealo-gies are produced to back up this claim. In Matthew, Joseph is addressed as "son of David," and indirectly the Davidic con-nection of Jesus is argued from his being born in Bethlehem, the city of David and expected birthplace of the Messiah. Presuming that in the original Semitic infancy story the Hebrew version of Isaiah 7:14 was used, it announced the birth of the coming redeemer called "God with us" or "Son of God," understood as the equivalent of Christ-Messiah yet without implying a virginal conception which could enter the picture only on the secondary Greek level. The two terms, Messiah and Son of God, are interconnected and automatically follow each other as in "You are the Christ, the Son of the living God" (Mt 16:16) or "Tell us if you are the Christ, the Son of God" (Mt 26:63). So in this reconstructed original Semitic version of the Infancy Gospel, Jesus, the son of Joseph of the house of David, is proclaimed the Christ surnamed Emmanuel (God with us) or in usual parlance the Messiah, Son of God.

The Semitic layer of the tradition subjacent to Luke con-tains the same messianic concept. Jesus, the son of Joseph of the house of David, is expected to inherit the royal throne and as Christ, the Lord, the Son of the Most High or the Son of God will reign over Israel forever. A miraculous element is at-tached to the story of Mary's conception without the support of a biblical quotation and without actually denying Joseph's participation in the process. The model introduced to explain the extraordinary happening is the humanly incomprehensible but biblically not unprecedented pregnancy of an aged woman, a "virgin for the second time." With Mary we seem to move in the opposite direction toward a pregnancy earlier than was thought possible and unparalleled in Scripture.

By the time the tradition reaches its Greek phase, thanks to the official Septuagint version of Isaiah 7 of the Greek-speaking Jews read with a Hellenistic mind-set, the original imagery evolves into the divinely enacted mystery of the virginal conception. The child thus produced is more and more perceived not just figuratively but literally as divine, a son fathered not by Joseph of the house of David, but by God himself through his Holy Spirit.

5. WHAT IS THE HISTORICAL VALUE AND THEOLOGICAL SIGNIFICANCE OF THE INFANCY GOSPELS?

From the nature of the birth stories and the many fabulous features incorporated in them—angels, dreams, virginal conception, miraculous star—one is forced to repeat the conclusion of W. D. Davies and D. C. Allison, namely, that the Infancy Gospels are "not the stuff out of which history is made" (see p. 14). However, some elements of history may be buried beneath legendary wrappings. They are admittedly basic, but they enjoy a high degree of probability when seen against the main Jesus story recorded in the subsequent sections of the Gospels. They testify to the birth of a Jewish child by the name of Jesus (Yeshua in Hebrew) to a couple called Mary (Miriam) and Joseph. The birth occurred according to both Matthew and Luke while Herod was king of Judaea (in or before 4 BC), and most likely during the end period of his reign. The location of the birth in Bethlehem, though firmly asserted in both accounts on theological grounds, is directly contradicted in John and indirectly in the Synoptics, where Galilee and Nazareth are designated as Jesus' home country and native town. On the other hand, both Matthew and Luke agree in pointing to Nazareth as the village where Jesus spent his youth. So if we were to reconstruct the birth certificate of Jesus, we could fill in the names and the place of residence of the child and the parents, but the date of birth could only be approximate, under Herod, and the locale controverted, Bethlehem according to tradition, but more likely Nazareth.

The doctrinal analysis of the Infancy Gospels shows that in their final stage of Greek development the central concepts of "Messiah–Redeemer" and "Son of God–God with us" are embedded in the miraculous atmosphere of the virginal conception and endowed with an enhanced theological content.

The essence of the joyful good tiding announced by the Nativity stories is that God has sent his Son, supernaturally born of a virgin mother, to save his people from their sins and bring peace to all men favored by God. This is the happy message that the Christian world identifies with Christmas. To achieve this, we have to apply a selective reading to the Infancy Gospels. The glorious Nativity of Church tradition is built on the sweet and simple story of Luke with angels, shepherds, and jolly neighbors. The merry Christmas that people

wish to one another is purged from the spoiling effects of the
Matthean drama with Joseph's psychological torture in face of
the dilemma of what to do with the pregnant Mary and the
fear, panic, and tears caused by Herod's edict threatening with
untimely extinction the budding life of the Son of God.

Notes

1   According to the theory advanced by the nineteenth-century German scholar Hermann Usener (*Das Weihnachtsfest*, 1889; 2nd ed. 1911), and developed by the Belgian Benedictine Dom Bernard Botte (*Les origines de la Noël et de l'Epiphanie*, 1932), the Nativity of Christ was assigned the date of the winter solstice, on which day the worshippers of the Persian god Mithra celebrated the birthday of the sun.

2   *Scottish Journal of Theology* 41 (1988), pp. 177–89.

3   *A Critical and Exegetical Commentary on the Gospel according to Saint Matthew* (Edinburgh), 1988, p. 252.

4   Ibid., p. 221.

5   *New York Review of Books*, June 29, 1978, pp. 39–42.

6   *The History of the Synoptic Tradition*, 1963, p. 291.

7   *The Historical Figure of Jesus* (London, 1993), p. 85.

8   "The Virginal Conception of Jesus in the New Testament," *Theological Studies* 34, 1973, pp. 566–67.

9   *To Advance the Gospel: New Testament Studies* (New York, 1981), pp. 61–62.

10   Curiously, the name Panthera/Pantera/Pandera is attested in the period as that borne by Roman soldiers, and epigraphic

evidence, dating to AD 9, refers to one particular Tiberius Julius Abdes *Pantera*, a Sidonian archer in a Roman legion stationed in far distant Germany. See A. Deissmann, "Der Name Panthera," *Orientalische Studien Th. Nöldecke gewid-met*, 1906, pp. 871–75. The possibility that Panthera was the father of Jesus has been revived by James D. Tabor in *The Jesus Dynasty* (Simon & Schuster, New York, 2006).

11   *Hitler's Table-Talk* (Oxford, 1988), pp. 76, 721.

12   See Jane Schaberg, *The Illegitimacy of Jesus* (Sheffield, 1995).

13   "The Titulus Tiburtinus," *Vestigia* 1972, Beiträge zur Alten Geschichte 17, Munich, p. 600.

14   See G. Ryckmans, "De l'or (?), de l'encens et de la myrrhe," *Revue Biblique* 58 (1951), pp. 372–76.

15   See Roger David Aus, *Matthew 1-2 and the Virginal Conception: In Light of Palestinian and Hellenistic Traditions on the Birth of Israel's First Redeemer, Moses* (University Press of America, 2004).

16   See Morton Smith, *Jesus the Magician* (Gollancz, London, 1978), pp. 46–50.

Select Bibliography

Aus, Roger David, *Matthew 1-2 and the Virginal Conception: In Light of Palestinian and Hellenistic Judaic Traditions on the Birth of Israel's First Redeemer, Moses* (University Press of America, Lanham, MD, 2004).

Brooke, George J., *The Dead Sea Scrolls and the New Testament* (SPCK, London, 2005), 262–64.

Brown, Raymond E., *The Virginal Conception and Bodily Resurrection of Jesus* (Paulist Press, New York, 1972).

———, *The Birth of the Messiah* (Doubleday, New York, 1993).

Bultmann, Rudolf, *The History of the Synoptic Tradition* (Blackwell, Oxford, 1963), 291–301.

Cullmann, Oscar, "The Origin of Christmas" in *The Early Church* (SCM, London, 1956), 17–36.

Davies, W. D., and Dale C. Allison, *The Gospel according to Saint Matthew, Volume I* [International Critical Commentary] (Edinburgh, 1988), 149–284.

Dunn, James D. G., *Jesus Remembered* (Eerdmans, Grand Rapids, 2003), 340–48.

Fitzmyer, Joseph A., *The Gospel according to Luke (I-IX)* (Doubleday, New York, 1981), 303–448.

————, "The Virginal Conception of Jesus in the New Testament" in *To Advance the Gospel* (Crossroad, New York, 1981), 41–79.

Gibson, Shimon, *The Cave of John the Baptist* (Arrow, London, 2005).

James, Montague Rhodes, *The Apocryphal New Testament* (Clarendon Press, Oxford, 1924).

Meier, John P., *A Marginal Jew, Volume I* (Doubleday, New York, 1991), 205–52.

Sanders, E. P., *The Historical Figure of Jesus* (Penguin, London, 1994), 80–91.

Schaberg, Jane, *The Illegitimacy of Jesus* (Crossroad, New York/Sheffield Academic Press, Sheffield, 1990/1995).

Schneemelcher, Wilhelm, *New Testament Apocrypha: Gospels and Related Writings* (Westminster John Knox Press, Nashville, 1991).

Smith, Morton, *Jesus the Magician* (Victor Gollancz, London, 1978), 24–28, 46–50.

Stauffer, Ethelbert, *Jesus and His Story* (SCM, London, 1960), 22–43.

Tabor, James D., *The Jesus Dynasty* (Simon & Schuster, New York, 2006).

Usener, Hermann, *Das Weihnachtsfest* (2nd ed., Friedrich Cohen, Bonn, 1911).

Vermes, Geza, *Jesus the Jew* (Collins/SCM Press, London 1973, 2001), 187–94.

————, *The Changing Faces of Jesus* (Penguin, London, 2001), 210–15.

Winter, Paul, "The Cultural Background for the Narrative in Luke I and II," *Jewish Quarterly Review* (1954), 159–67, 230–42, 287.

Index